Partitioned Freedom

Partitioned Freedom

Ram Madhav

PRABHAT PAPERBACKS

Published by
PRABHAT PAPERBACKS
An imprint of Prabhat Prakashan Pvt. Ltd.
4/19 Asaf Ali Road,
New Delhi-110002 (INDIA)
e-mail: prabhatbooks@gmail.com

ISBN 978-93-5521-244-3
PARTITIONED FREEDOM
by Shri Ram Madhav

Edition
First, 2022

Price
₹ 350.00 (Rupees Three Hundred Fifty only)

Printed at
R-Tech Offset Printers, Delhi

Contents

Foreword

So much has been written about partition of India in the last seven decades. That literature included books authored by scholars on both the sides – India and Pakistan. In fact, more literature emanated from Pakistan than India. Many foreign scholars too contributed to this research and documentation.

'Partitioned Freedom' is an addition to that existing literature on the tragedy of humungous proportions. Facts being facts, the only liberty that an author can take while working on much-used themes like this one will be to provide a perspective from his or her own vantage point.

As a young college student and subsequently a social activist, I had read a few books on India's partition that intrigued me greatly. They included books by authors like H.V. Seshadri, B.R. Nanda, Raj Mohan Gandhi, Khan Abdul Wali Khan and Ram Manohar Lohia.They provided different perspectives about that tragic history of India's vivisection. But one common factor was that none had defended partition.

That question bothered me always. None, except Jinnah and his coterie, wanted Pakistan. Many Muslim leaders were also opposed to it. Yet it could not be prevented.

The Two-Nation Theory of Jinnah, which was the basis

on which creation of a separate homeland for Muslims was sought, was a fragile and lacklustre theory. Intellectually it was hollow. It was far removed from the objective reality. Jinnah's argument that India's Muslims, apart from their differences with Hindus, had a common identity was a facile one. Muslims lived all across India. There couldn't have been a homeland for all the Indian Muslims except of course a mammoth exercise of exchange of population. Jinnah and Ambedkar talked about it, but both probably knew it was not an easy proposition.

Still Jinnah succeeded in raking up temporary emotions and mobilising majority Muslim opinion in his favour. Its fallacy was proven on the day India was partitioned. Of the hundred million, only a half of the Muslim population went over to Pakistan. Rest remained in India, either out of compulsion – they couldn't afford a migration, or out of choice – they didn't support partition. In just two decades time, the much-touted Two-Nation Theory returned to haunt Pakistan when the Bengali-speaking Muslims of Pakistan wanted their own homeland and secured it in 1971 in the form of Bangladesh. Hindustan was divided on Two-Nation Theory in 1947, and Pakistan was divided on the same theory in 1971. Poetic justice.

However fictitious the theory may be, it has not only divided the territory, but also hearts. A deep division of hearts, created by partition, continues to trouble the two communities in South Asia. In the Constituent Assembly in August 1947, Jinnah promised a country where the minorities would have equal rights as the majority. But that speech was intended to please the Americans and other western audience. What Pakistan came to represent was a quintessential theocracy. Jinnah knew well that there was nothing else that could keep the country together except Islam. To that was added 'hate India'. The country that Jinnah created out of the Two-Nation Theory can only survive by promoting theocracy and hating India.

History cannot be reversed. But it can be prevented from repeating. Partition of India is not just history, nor a sob story. It has lessons for posterity. It is not just about the hypothesis as to whether it could have been prevented. It is about whether another partition can knock at India's doors and how such a calamity can be prevented.

India's freedom movement was a historic saga about which every Indian should have great reverence. All those who contributed to India's freedom continue to be cherished as national heroes and martyrs with utmost respect. Analysis of certain historical facts and events shouldn't be construed as demeaning the contribution of any of our great freedom fighters.

I authored a book on India's Partition in Telugu in 1990. With my little life experience of just two-and-half decades, I couldn't fully comprehend the enormity of the subject. Three decades later, I am better read and better informed. Consistency is the virtue of the dead. One should be consistent only with truth, as Gandhi used to say. I came across many new facts over the course of last three decades based on which I decided to come out with this new book.

Indian Government has, for the first time, acknowledged in 2021 that the horrors of partition must be revisited in order to learn lessons from it. That prompted me to write a series of eight articles in India Foundation's Chintan online forum of public opinion in 2021. This book is an expansion of that thought.

Will the partition end? Will Akhand Bharat be achieved? These questions are relevant for many. But the bigger and more important question should be about the division of hearts rather than territory. Can the legacy of partition in the form of division of hearts between Hindus and Muslims end? Can they live together as one nation? Or Jinnah's ghost will continue to haunt us forever?

I must acknowledge the hardwork put in by Shubhrastha, who is like my niece and Deeksha, who is like my daughter in preparing the manuscript for publication in record time. They deserve praise for this book seeing the light in a short time.

Hope the readers find it useful.

August 14, 2022 **—Ram Madhav**

Nobody Wanted it But Nobody Stood Up

The idea of two nationalities in India is only a new-fangled notion invented by Jinnah for his purposes and contrary to the facts. More than 90% of the Indian Mussulmans are descendants of converted Hindus and belong as much to the Indian nation as the Hindus themselves.

—*Rishi Aurobindo*

It was the 15th of August. The year was 1947.

It was the midnight of the intervening night of August 14-15, to be more precise.

Those were the exact moments when India was declared independent. Those were the sacred moments when the Indian nation had unshackled itself from the slavery of a millennium and relished the fragrance of freedom.

Naturally there were jubilations and celebrations everywhere. No Indian had slept that night. They were all on the streets, cheering, chanting and celebrating the 'victory of Mother Bharat'. Slogans of "*Bharat Mata ki Jai*" reverberated in the nook and corner of the country. There were endless revelries across the length and breadth of the country on that night – from the streets of Delhi and North India to the mood, tired after the day-long fasting and prayers.

"I cannot rejoice on August 15. I do not want to deceive you. But at the same time, I shall not ask you not to rejoice. Unfortunately, the kind of freedom we have got today contains also the seeds of future conflict between India and Pakistan," he told his colleagues in July that year.[2]

* * *

Gandhi no doubt was prophetic about the future conflict. But what was the 'kind of freedom' that had put him off?

India's Independence was a moment of jubilation and pride for over 350 million Indians. Although a few leaders tried to appropriate the credit for it by claiming that it was they who were responsible for it, India's Independence movement saw the participation of many different parties and groups with disparate ideologies coming together with the singular objective of removing the British rule and establishing self-rule. The mainstream movement was led by the Indian National Congress under the leadership of stalwarts like Gandhi, Nehru, Sardar Patel and others. Their contribution was significant and substantial.

But there were other streams too, that didn't fully share the mainstream movement's ideology of 'non-violent resistance'. As the erudite Sanskrit scholar from Nagpur, Bal Shastri Hardas highlights in his revealing book, *Armed Struggle for Freedom–1857 to Subhash*, there was a parallel campaign of violent struggles that continued alongside the peaceful Congress movement. It involved a large number of revolutionaries like Bhagat Singh, Chandrashekhar Azad and Ashfaqullah Khan, who had laid down their lives pursuing revolutionary path against the brutal British empire. There were also leaders like Swatantra Veer Vinayak Damodar

Savarkar who used their pen to inspire a generation of revolutionary warriors.

Finally, the Azad Hind Fauj or the Indian National Army (INA) of Netaji Subhas Chandra Bose hit the last nail on the British coffin in the final years of the Independence struggle. In a scintillating address to the Indians at a rally in Burma (present day Myanmar), Netaji gave the clarion call asking for greater sacrifices to obtain Independence from the British. "We should have but one desire today – the desire to die so that India may live; the desire to face a martyr's death, so that the path to freedom may be paved with the martyrs' blood. Friends! My comrades in the War of Liberation! Today, I demand of you of one thing, above all. I demand of you, blood. It is blood alone that can avenge the blood that the enemy has spilt. It is blood alone that can pay the price of freedom," he said.

He ended his address with a thunderous appeal, "Give me blood and I promise you freedom."

Soldiers of the INA entered the Indian soil by crossing the Indo-Burmese border in Manipur, in early 1944. With the help of the Japanese soldiers, they defeated the British Army and liberated a large chunk of territory in present-day Manipur and Nagaland. The Azad Hind flag was hoisted by Lt. Col. Shaukat Ali Malik on April 14, 1944 at Moirang, in Manipur,[3] which acted as the headquarters of the INA for the next three months until it was recaptured by the British and a large number of INA soldiers were arrested.

INA's adventurous battles and the capture of Moirang triggered a new wave of enthusiasm and spirit in the Indian masses, who were disheartened by the failure of the Quit India call given by Gandhi in 1942. The fire and frenzy lit by the INA was so fierce that rebellions broke out in the Royal British Army and Navy with the Indian soldiers, who constituted the majority in the armed forces, refusing to obey the orders of their British officers.

The rebels, who started calling themselves the Indian National Navy, on the lines of Netaji's INA, mutinied initially at Bombay (now Mumbai) in 1946, but the unrest soon spread from Karachi to Calcutta (now Kolkata). It involved over twenty thousand sailors and seventy-eight ships. The British government tried to suppress the revolt by deploying British troops and Royal Navy warships. But ultimately, it was the intervention of Sardar Patel upon the request of the British government that led to the end of the rebellion.

At the peak of the agitation, sections of the Royal Indian Air Force and Royal Indian Army too joined the revolt. There were incidents of unrest in the army contingents of Madras and Poona (called Chennai and Pune, respectively now) with the soldiers deliberately defying the orders of their British superiors and offering salute with their left hands in a mark of revolt. Occasional rioting and unrest too were reported.

One important trigger for the naval revolt was the public trial of the INA officers that was initiated at Delhi's Red Fort in May 1945 by the British. Although ideologically opposed to violent struggles, the Indian National Congress leadership too saw in the INA trials an opportunity to re-ignite the spirit of freedom among the masses and came forward to defend the INA soldiers, like Shah Nawaz Khan, Prem Sahgal, Gurbaksh Singh Dhillon, Abdul Rashid, Shinghara Singh, Fateh Khan and Captain Malik Munawar Khan Awan. The defence team deployed by the Congress included prominent legal luminaries, like Bhulabhai Desai, Asaf Ali, Sharat

Chandra Bose, Tej Bahadur Sapru, Kailash Nath Katju and Lt. Col. Horilal Varma. Even Jawaharlal Nehru, who had by then become an ardent advocate of Gandhi's non-violence, jumped into the defence of INA soldiers at the Red Fort. Taking out his black coat, which he relinquished in 1922 when he decided to give up his lucrative legal profession in favour of devoting full time to the freedom struggle, Nehru joined his colleagues occasionally at the Red Fort trials.

Bal Shastri Hardas infers that it was these revolutionary struggles that eventually rattled the British Empire into surrendering before the Indian freedom struggle and grant Independence. He cites the debates in the British House of Commons in the second half of 1946 in support of his inference.

Winston Churchill, who lost the election and became the leader of the opposition in the British Parliament by then, was fiercely opposed to granting freedom to India. Indians were incapable of ruling themselves, he argued, opposing Prime Minister Clement Atlee's proposal for granting Independence. "Power will go into the hands of rascals, rogues and freebooters. Not a bottle of water or loaf of bread shall escape taxation; only the air will be free and the blood of these hungry millions will be on the head of Attlee," he disparagingly said of Indian leaders.[4] Atlee's defence of his decision is worth revisiting to understand Hardas' contention. Atlee didn't talk about the Quit India movement launched by the Congress. The two principal reasons that he enumerated in defence of his decision to grant Independence to India were: one, that the Indian soldiers of the Royal Indian Army were no longer loyal to the British officers, and second, the British Army could no longer afford to send a large contingent of British soldiers to far off lands, like India, especially after the bloody experience of the Second World War.

Eminent historian R.C. Mazumdar also argues in his book "Three Phases of India's Struggle for Freedom" that it was not the non-violent mass movement that brought freedom but a "series of global factors". He was even prepared to credit "the humanity of British imperialism" before Ahimsa as the bringer of independence[5].

Besides these revolutionaries and non-violent *satyagrahis*, many others too had contributed their bit to India's freedom. Saints, sages, litterateurs, farmers and forest-dwellers – every section of Indian society contributed to that gigantic movement. Women played an important role, so did the royals of many princely states. Industrialists, like Jamnalal Bajaj and Jamshedji Tata too had risked the anger of the British rulers to support the Independence movement.

Jamshedji Tata needs special mention. Once Jamshedji went to Britain where a friend invited him to meet at Watson's Hotel. When Jamshedji reached the hotel, he was not allowed to enter it because the hotel was exclusively for 'Whites Only'. The manager told him that Indians were not allowed in the hotel. Jamshedji Tata took it as an insult to all Indians and went on to build an iconic hotel in Mumbai, which became the Taj Mahal Hotel, near the Gateway of India. He also took it as a challenge to start those industries for which India was dependent on British imports. He started textile mills in Nagpur and the famous steel manufacturing mill in Jamshedpur. He made sure that the machinery for those mills was not imported from England, but instead, from Germany. Long before the *swadeshi* movement was launched by the Congress in 1905, Jamshedji Tata had already actualised it in his industrial activity.

India's Independence was the cumulative result of all such efforts by disparate forces through different means and methods.

* * *

A moment of joy for 400 million Indians also became a moment of sorrow and suffering for several millions among them. While granting Independence, the British had partitioned India into two, in a hurried manner to create Pakistan as a separate nation. Overnight, for those several millions, the land under their feet, on which they had lived for generations, became foreign. Millions found themselves on the wrong side of what was to be their future home. Not unexpectedly, massive violence broke out on both sides of the clumsily carved-out frontiers.

Some leaders tried to defend the Partition of the country, arguing that it was like "brothers apportioning their property". Brothers can apportion property, but not their mother. Country is not just a piece of territory; it is a mother – the motherland. Once a Muslim woman accosted Gandhi and asked "if two brothers were living together in the same house and wanted to separate and live in different houses, would you object"? "Yes", Gandhi replied, "If they wanted to weaken the foundation of the old house and hasten its destruction"[6].

The Partition was not a smooth and peaceful affair either. India was partitioned over the dead bodies of hundreds of thousands of innocents. Historians wrote poignantly that the Sindhu (Indus) river flowed not with water, but with the blood of tens of thousands of Hindus and Muslims. "Across the sub-continent, communities that had co-existed for almost a millennium attacked each other in a terrifying outbreak of sectarian violence, with Hindus and Sikhs on one side and Muslims on the other – a mutual genocide as unexpected as it was unprecedented. In Punjab and Bengal– provinces abutting India's borders with West and East Pakistan, respectively – the carnage was especially intense, with massacres, arson, forced conversions, mass abductions and savage sexual violence. Some seventy-five thousand women were raped, and many of them were then disfigured or dismembered", wrote historian William Dalrymple in an article in *The New Yorker* magazine.[7]

Dalrymple also quoted Nisid Hajari, the author of Midnight's Furies – a "fast-paced new narrative history of Partition and its aftermath", as saying, "Gangs of killers set whole villages aflame, hacking to death men and children and the aged while carrying off young women to be raped. Some British soldiers and journalists, who had witnessed the Nazi death camps, claimed Partition's brutalities were worse: pregnant women had their breasts cut off and babies hacked out of their bellies; infants were found literally roasted on spits."[8]

Millions were uprooted and leaving everything behind, forced to undertake an arduous and often hazardous trek of hundreds of miles, seeking a new home and meaning to live. Not all could reach their destinations. Waylaid, raped and murdered, many unlucky ones perished on the way to the destination that they never chose. A year later, when the forced migrations came to an end, over fifteen million people had been uprooted from their homes and hearths, while the number of dead was estimated to be anywhere between one to two million.

People remember the Holocaust and the wanton

migration of millions of Jews into the newly formed state of Israel, but, the world hardly knew about the genocidal Partition of India, leading to forced migration of millions. "It was the world's largest and rarest exodus," wrote Larry Collins and Dominique Lapierre in their famous book on India's Partition, *Freedom at Midnight*.

In his book, *Negationism in India – Concealing the Record of Islam*, Koenraad Elst, a Belgian historian of Indology, says: "The number of victims of the persecutions of Hindus by Muslims is of the same order of magnitude as that of the Nazi extermination policy, though no one has yet made the effort of tabulating the reported massacres and proposing a reasonable estimate of how many millions exactly must have died in the course of the Islamic campaign against Hinduism."[9]

Why did this tragedy take place? Who was responsible?

None of the leading lights of India's Independence movement wanted India to be divided; neither did the majority of people of India – both Muslim and Hindu.

"Vivisect me before vivisecting India,"[10] Gandhi warned firmly, when he was informed about the Muslim League's Lahore Resolution of March 24, 1940 in which it demanded that the "areas in which the Muslims are numerically in a majority, as in the north-western and eastern zones of India should be grouped to constitute 'independent states' in which the constituent units should be autonomous and sovereign."[11] Although the word 'Pakistan' was not used, the reference to 'autonomous and sovereign independent states' made the intentions of the League amply clear. They were demanding a separate country. This resolution became popular later in the history as 'Pakistan Resolution'.

For Gandhi, the Pakistan resolution was a 'moral sin'. It militated against all his lifelong convictions, especially his dearest idea of Hindu-Muslim unity. It was totally unacceptable to him. "The step of Mr. Jinnah is like that two brothers have a fight on same cow and they cut it and divide it," he lamented. Yet the country was divided in front of his eyes.

Jawaharlal Nehru, in his typical romantic way, proclaimed that the idea of Partition was a 'fantastic nonsense', meaning 'the fantasy of some mad people'. Yet he became one of the signatories of the 'June 3rd Plan' for the country's Partition. Sardar Patel went one step further and declared in his typical style: "*Talwar se talwar bhidegi*" (sword will clash with sword), meaning that the countrymen would fight till the end against Partition. But he became a mute witness to the passing of the 'June 3rd Plan'.

Dr. Rajendra Prasad, who was in jail during the Quit India movement, went on to write the book, *India Divided,* in which he highlighted the ills of Partition and how illogical the thought was. The book was published in early 1946. Even before the ink on the pages dried up, India was partitioned.

Rishi Aurobindo was deeply disturbed by Partition and insisted that 'it must go'. "The old communal division into Hindus and Muslims seems now to have hardened into a permanent political division of the country. It is to be hoped that this settled fact will not be accepted as settled forever or as anything more than a temporary expedient. For, if it lasts, India may be seriously weakened, even crippled: civil strife may remain always possible; possibly even a new invasion and foreign conquest. India's internal development and prosperity may be impeded; her position among the nations weakened; her destiny impaired, or even frustrated," he warned, quite prophetically.[12]

Even a hardened communist like C. Achutha Menon too described Partition as a negation of the cultural and territorial integrity of India of the ages. Socialist leader Ram Manohar Lohia's opposition to it is well known and so is that of others like Jayaprakash Narayan, Acharya Kripalani and Syama Prasad Mookerjee. Talking of Savarkar's opposition to Partition, Dr. B.R. Ambedkar writes: "As defined by Savarkar, Hindu Mahasabha is against Pakistan and proposes to resist it by all means. Mr. Jinnah says India should be cut up into two – Pakistan and Hindustan – but Mr. Savarkar insists that India shall not be divided into two parts."

Not just the Indian leaders, many British leaders toodid not support the idea of partitioning India. Lord Wavell, who was the British Viceroy, during 1943-47, opposed it in 1944, stating, "India is a God-made triangle; you cannot divide it." At the time of the Bangladesh war, *New Statesman*, a popular British tabloid, commented that Pakistan's creation was "territorially and culturally inappropriate". It called Pakistan "a State that never was."

Even the British Prime Minister Clement Atlee's original mandate as Britain's Prime Minister to Lord Mountbatten, who was sent to Delhi to replace Lord Wavell in February 1947, was not to Partition India. "Keep it united if possible. Save a bit from the wreck. Bring the British out in any case," was Attlee's instruction to Mountbatten.[13]

Yet the country was partitioned.

What became Pakistan was not just an ordinary piece of land; it was the sacred beliefs, customs and traditions of millions of Hindus that were ruthlessly partitioned. If India was the mother of the *Vedas*, it was on the banks of River Sindhu that those *Vedas* were organised and articulated.

That sacred land of the *Vedas* was given away into the hands of the enemies of the Vedic civilisation. Panini was a great grammarian who had authored standard grammar for Sanskrit language. His birthplace became Pakistan. The kingdom of *Hiranyakashyapa*, the sacred playground of Prahlada, the place where Lord Vishnu had descended in the *avatar* of Narasimha – half-man and half-lion – called in ancient history as Moolasthan, went to Pakistan and became Multan. Lahore, a city believed to have been built by Luv, son of Bhagwan Ram, which was also the capital city of the great Sikh warrior-king Maharaja Ranjit Singh, became the capital of Pakistan. Tragedy is, it was in this city, on the banks of River Ravi, that the Congress passed its historic resolution for 'total independence' in 1929, rejecting efforts of the British and the League to create divisions in the Indian society.

Takshashila, the ancient university of global repute, where Acharya Chanakya had taught as a teacher, became Taxila in Pakistan. Ancient cities of the great Indus Valley civilisation, which imparted a unique identity to the Indic civilisation, were no longer in India.

At least, was Partition done rationally? The major forest cover in Punjab and Bengal went to India. Pakistan was bereft of coal and needed to depend on India for it. Orissa and Bihar (now Jharkhand) had all the reserves of iron ore and steel factories, while East Pakistan had none. Pakistan had surplus power and India faced shortage. Jute cultivation was happening in East Pakistan while all jute mills were located in Kolkata. There were thirty textile mills in undivided Bengal and out of these only seven went to East Pakistan while the rest remained in India.

After Partition, sharing of waters became a bone of contention between India and Pakistan initially and continues to trouble bilateral relations between India, Pakistan and Bangladesh. Both Pakistan and Bangladesh have complained on international fora that India was waging water wars against them and "killing them by thirst". It gives us a glimpse of how much inconvenience Partition had caused to both sides.

Partition had not only created two countries, but two enemies. Security concerns started dominating the policies of both the governments immediately after Partition. Both had to spend billions of dollars for securing their borders. Many studies by international agencies concluded that had the amount of money spent on security been utilised for developmental work, the human development indices in both countries would have seen greater progress.

Partition brought immediate sufferings and long-term misery to both sides.

* * *

Nehru used to say that those who forget history are condemned to repeat it. But he never seemed to have learnt any lessons from this tragic history. Neither he nor his successors allowed the truth of this tragedy to be told to the generations nor did they sensitise them about the blunders committed in history. It was a tragic and horrific history, prompting a commentator to quip insultingly that "India's freedom was a bargained freedom".

It is an exaggeration and insult to great freedom fighters of India to call it a bargain. Nevertheless, there was a history of bargain in the Partition of India, very little about which has been written or talked about. Talking about that tragedy was considered politically incorrect and anti-secular. It was only after many decades, when the relations between the countries touched their nadir, pushing the world to the brink of a nuclear war, did some debate over Partition and its fallacy begin prominently.

India had paid as much a price for hiding the horrors of the Partition as for the Partition itself. India's territorial integrity continued to be threatened by forces from within as much as without. Minority communalism not only continued but was rewarded in the name of distorted notions of secularism. Despite horrific experiences of Partition, Hindus and Muslims today remain as aloof and insulated as they were before the Partition.

Revisiting horrors of the Partition is needed not just as an academic exercise, nor to hate anybody, but to learn appropriate lessons and avoid another Partition .

* * *

One of the first voices of dissent was that of the renowned socialist leader and thinker, Ram Manohar Lohia. In his book, *The Guilty Men of India's Partition*, Lohia enumerates who he considers as the essential players responsible for the tragedy. "....First the British chicanery, secondly, declining years of Congress leadership, thirdly, objective condition of Hindu-Muslim rioting, fourthly, lack of grit and stamina among the people, fifthly, Gandhi's non-violence, sixthly, Muslim League's separatism, seventhly, inability to seize opportunities as they came, and, rightly, Hindu hauteur," Lohia wrote.[14] In his opinion, the principal players were Gandhi, Jinnah and Mountbatten.

Mountbatten presented the final plan for India's Partition to the leaders of the Congress and the Muslim League in a meetingon June 3, 1947. It is famously called as the 'June 3rd Plan'. Jawaharlal Nehru, Sardar Patel and Acharya Kripalani were present on behalf of the Congress while the Muslim League was represented by Muhammad Ali Jinnah, Liaquat Ali Khan and Abdur Nishtar. Mountbatten later claimed that "the Indian leaders agreed unanimously, without any sort of reservation, to the choice of 15th August."[15]

When the 'June 3rd plan' for Partition was placed before the Congress Working Committee on June 14, 1947, it encountered stiff opposition from the members. Curiously, Gandhi, who declared six years before that it could only happen over his dead body, intervened to ask the members to support the Partition. Agreeing that he was one of those who steadfastly opposed the division of India, Gandhi, nevertheless, urged the members to accept the resolution as "sometimes certain decisions, however unpalatable they might be, had to be taken". Gandhi indicated that if the resolution was rejected, they would have to find a "new set of leaders". He also insisted that it was essential for peace in the country.

While nobody wanted Partition of India, nobody was there to stand up against it when the moment came. It needed people to come on to the streets to fight with the forces of vivisection as also the leaders to lead that resistance. Unfortunately, at that momentous juncture, people were not ready to fight to save India's integrity – they lacked "grit and stamina" as Lohia put it[16], and the leaders were in "declining years". "We became old," one of them confessed later.

Reference—

1. *Nehru, Jawaharlal (1947): A Tryst with Destiny. Source: https://archive.org/details/HindSwaraj-Speech-03-1*
2. *Akbar, M.J. (2019): Gandhi's Hinduism – The Struggle Against Jinnah's Islam,Bloomsbury Publishing*
3. *Prime Minister's Secretariat, Netaji Subhas Chandra Bose Declassified Files. Accessible at https://archive.org/stream/netaji/284_djvu.txt*
4. *Churchill Project, Churchill on India. Accessible at https://winstonchurchill.hillsdale.edu/churchill-on-india/*
5. *Matthews Roderick, "Jinnah Vs. Gandhi" pp. 243, Hachette India*
6. *Zakaria, Rafiq (1999), "Gandhi and the Break-Up of India" pp. 227, Bharatiya Vidya Bhavan*
7. *Dalrymple, William (June 22, 2015): The Great Divide – The Violent Legacy of Indian Partition,The New Yorker*
8. *Ibid*
9. *Elst, Koenraad (1992): Negationism in India: Concealing the Record of Islam, p. 7, The Voice of India, New Delhi, India*
10. *Mazumdar, Bharati (2002): Gandhiji on Partition, p. 1, Mani Bhavan Gandhi Sangrahalaya, Mumbai*
11. *Jalal, Ayesha (1985): The Sole Spokesman: Jinnah, the Muslim League and the Demand for Pakistan, p. 58, Cambridge University Press, Great Britain*
12. *Sri Aurobindo's message at the request of All India Radio, Tiruchirappalli, for broadcast on the eve of India's Independence,'The 15th of August 1947 Message by Sri Aurobindo'. Accessible at https://aurosociety.org/society/index/1947%2C-August-15th-Message*
13. *Ziegler, Philip (1985): Mountbatten, p. 359, Williams Collins, Great Britain*
14. *Lohia, Ram Manohar (1960): Guilty Men of India's Partition, p. 7, Kitabistan, Allahabad, Uttar Pradesh, India*
15. *Basu, Narayani (2020): V.P. Menon: The Unsung Architect of Modern India, p. 426, Simon and Schuster*
16. *Lohia, Ram Manohar (1960): Guilty Men of India's Partition, p. 7, Kitabistan, Allahabad, Uttar Pradesh, India*

□

Divide Et Impera Defeated

Our nation is like a tree of which the original trunk is swarajya and the branches are swadeshi and boycott.

—Bal Gangadhar Tilak

India's Partition was essentially based on the premise that Hindus and Muslims constituted two separate nations, and they could not live together as one community. Mohammad Ali Jinnah, leader of the Muslim League, was the loudest in arguing for a separate homeland for Indian Muslims.

Islam knocked at the shores of India in early 8th century AD, in less than hundred years of the passing of the Prophet in AD 632. In AD 711, Mohammad bin Qasim, the General sent by the Arab Governor of Basra, attacked the kingdom of Raja Dahir, the last Hindu king of the remote north-western region of Sindh. There were a couple of attacks from the Arabs earlier too, but Dahir's armies could successfully repel them. But when Qasim came with a large army and several of Dahir's subordinates started surrendering, Dahir himself moved to the battle-front to stall Qasim from crossing the Sindhu River. He knew that he was the only wall between the kingdoms of India and the Arab invaders.

In a fierce battle, despite his stiff resistance, Dahir failed to stop Qasim from crossing the river and eventually became a martyr in the battle. Qasim mutilated the body of Dahir in a cruel manner unknown to the Indian region and sent his severed head to the Governor of Basra as a victory monument.

The next eight centuries saw waves of Muslim invaders from Arab, Turkish and Central Asian regions into the Indian mainland. Invasions across the Hindu Kush Mountain range were not new to India. Greeks, Huns, Kushans and Shakas came from the west and waged battles with the native kings. These were essentially political and economic in nature. The invaders either went back with their booty or mingled with the native society seamlessly.

But the Islamic invasions were different in the sense that they brought religion also with them. They reached Delhi by the end of the 11th century and proceeded further down, up to Tamil Nadu and Karnataka. The medieval Islam that these invaders brought with them was exclusivist, intolerant and iconoclastic. Religions of India, seeped in a tradition of tolerance and inclusivity, had a very open worldview. These were confronted with and overawed by the opposite tenets of the new religion.

Islamic invasions also resulted in a large number of native Hindu population converted to Islam, either through inducements or through political negotiations or, in many cases, through force. "The Islamic conquest of India is probably the bloodiest story in history," wrote eminent American author, historian and philosopher Will Durant.[1] Court chroniclers of the invading rulers had recorded about the acute mistrust and animosity that existed between the people of native religions and those who had converted to Islam. They lived insular lives. Hindus were subjected to unjust levies, like *jazia* (tax). Cow was sacred to Hindus, but cow slaughter became the order under Islamic rule. Temples were destroyed; women subjected to atrocities; and Hindus, in general, lived like second-class citizens. Unlike the invaders in the past , Islamic invaders never tried to mingle with the native Hindu society.

Al-Biruni, the Iranian scholar, who came to India with the invading armies of Mahmood Ghaznavi in the early 11th century and stayed back in India to study Sanskrit and Hinduism, gives a glimpse of the sense of Islamic superiority that the invading hordes brought with them. "We have here given an account of these things in order that the reader may learn by the comparative treatment of the subject how much superior the institutions of Islam are, and how more plainly this contrast brings out all customs and usages, differing from those of Islam, in their essential foulness," he wrote pompously.[2] Dismissing Hindus for "their ludicrous views", Al-Biruni disparagingly says: "The Hindus believe that there is no country but theirs, no nation like theirs, no kings like theirs, no religion like theirs, no science like theirs. They are haughty, foolishly vain, self-conceited and stolid. They are by nature niggardly..."[3] Al-Biruni also admits that because of the raids by Mahmud of Ghazni, Hindus "cherish the most inveterate aversion toward all Muslims."[4]

Next several centuries saw this distance grow between the two communities. Nearly three centuries later, in the 14th century, Ibn Batuta, an explorer and traveller in the Islamic lands, observed that Hindus and Muslims lived in entirely separate communities. From his experience of Malabar region, he remarked that Hindus neither allowed intermarriage with Muslims, nor entertained inter-dining. "It is the custom among the heathen of the Malabar country that no Muslim should enter their houses or use their vessels for eating purposes. If a Muslim is fed out of their vessels, they either break the vessels or give them away to the Muslims," Batuta wrote.[5]

B.R. Nanda, eminent author and the biographer of Gandhi, quotes an unknown Turkish author to say that "Allah and Mohammad could not be accommodated in the Hindu pantheon, nor were Muslims absorbed in Hindu society as a caste."[6]

* * *

But as centuries passed and the invasions started bringing shrunk dividends, relations between the two communities saw some improvement. Emperor Jehangir's mother was a Hindu. Jehangir's Hindu wife gave birth to his successor Emperor Shah Jahan. Aurangzeb had a Hindu wife too. The last Mughal ruler, Bahadur Shah Zafar's mother Lal Bai was a Hindu. Some members of the Mughal royalty, like Akbar and Dara Shikoh demonstrated an element of syncretism in their actions and approach. Emperor Akbar is credited with setting up an establishment at Fatehpur Sikri for translating Indian scriptures and getting the epic *Mahabharata* translated into Persian and called it *Razmnama* (Book of Wars). Dara Shikoh, the Mughal crown prince and the brother of religious bigot Aurangzeb, had the *Bhagvad Gita* translated into Persian. He composed a study of Hinduism and Islam, called *The Mingling of Two Oceans*, which highlighted the commonalities in both the religions.

Then came the rule of Aurangzeb, one of the harshest and bloodiest chapters in Hindu-Muslim relations. Even historians, who are generally sympathetic about the Mughal rule in India, too could not whitewash the evil deeds of

Aurangzeb. They all agree that Aurangzeb had reversed the policies of Akbar as far as religious amity was concerned and pursued the policy of Islamic domination.

Renowned British Orientalist, Stanley Lane-Poole, wrote, "For the first time in their history, the Mughals beheld a rigid Muslim in their emperor – a Muslim as sternly repressible of himself as of his people around him; a king who was prepared to stake his throne for the sake of his faith. He must have been fully conscious of the dangerous path he was pursuing, and well aware against every Hindu sentiment. Yet he chose this course and adhered to this with unbending resolve through close on fifty years of unchallenged sovereignty."[7]

Even Dr. S.R. Sharma, a Left-leaning historian, writing about the acts of religious intolerance of Aurangzeb, observed, "These were not the acts of a righteous ruler or constructive statesman, but the outbursts of blind fanaticism, unworthy of the great genius that Aurangzeb undoubtedly possessed in all other aspects."

Despite their insistence, the Muslim rulers could not fully influence the behaviour and practices of the poorer sections of the Muslim masses, who constituted more than eighty percent of their population. As the Mughal rule declined, rural Muslims started returning to their old Hindu practices. Poor Muslims, especially in provinces like Bengal, were as caste-ridden as their Hindu counterparts. They also used to worship Goddess Kali and participate in Durga Puja. The *British Census Report* of 1901 noted that the poor and uneducated Muslims used to consult astrologers, look for auspicious days to start any work, and prayed to Hindu deities for all sorts of personal problems. Some of the Muslim communities in the princely states of Rajasthan, like the Meos, who converted to Islam during imperial wars between the Rajputs and the Mughals, used to even celebrate Hindu festivals like Diwali, Dussehra and Janmashtami.

In North India, a new and syncretic Islam started taking roots. Broadly called as Sufism, this tradition accommodated many Hindu practices like tolerance, saint-worship and *Dargah* and Idgah worship.

Decline of the Mughal Empire in India coincided with the decline of Islamic domination in Europe and the rise of Imperial powers in the Asian continent. The last and beleaguered Mughal Emperor Bahadur Shah Zafar, who came to the throne in 1837, once again tried to restore Hindu-Muslim bonhomie during his regime in the 19th century as he believed that Hinduism and Islam "share the same essence". He filled his court and army with a large number of Hindus. In his path-breaking work on the Mutiny of 1857, which he rechristened as the 'First War of Independence', V.D. Savarkar wrote in exuberant terms about Zafar's enthroning. "So, in the truer sense, we said that the raising of Bahadur Shah to the throne of India was no restoration at all. But rather, it was the declaration that the long-standing war between the Hindu and the Mohammedan had ended, that tyranny had ceased, and that the people of the soil were once more free to choose their own monarch. For, Bahadur Shah was raised by the free voice of the people, both Hindus and Mohammedans, civil and military, to be their Emperor and the head of the War of Independence. Therefore, on the 11th of May, this old venerable Bahadur Shah was not the old Mogul succeeding to the throne of Akbar or Aurangzeb, but he was the freely chosen monarch of a people battling for freedom against a foreign intruder. Let, then, Hindus and Mohammedans send forth their hearty, conscientious, and most loyal homage to this elected or freely accepted Emperor of their native soil on the 11th of May 1857!"[8]

* * *

This growing syncretism, together with the new-found bonhomie was there in ample evidence at the time of the First War of Independence in 1857, which the British had disparagingly described as the Sepoy Mutiny. Savarkar also regarded the battles of 1857 as a glorious period of the unity among Hindus and Muslims.

The revolt of 1857 shook the British confidence. They realised that a potential opposition to their rule was building up in the unity of various sections of the Indian society. George William Forrest, a British educator, had authored a book on the revolt and titled, *A History of the Indian Mutiny*. He warned the British Government that the message of the 1857 revolt was that the Hindus, Muslims, Brahmins and Shudras could all come together unitedly against the British Raj.

The Queen of England had designated October 7, 1857 as the 'National Humiliation Day' to express public concern over the sad state of affairs in India. The British were so rattled that calls for revenge started appearing in mainstream media, in London. Some suggested that "Delhi be razed to the ground, its puppet king publicly tried and found guilty and publicly executed." Even a respected paper, like *The Times*, started publishing provocative statements like the one by Vicar William Dews, who called upon his countrymen to "punish to death every Sepoy who has been accessory to the murder of any officer or civilian."[9]

Reprisal by the British soldiers over the defeated mutineers began after these public calls for revenge. Indian soldiers and their relatives were brutally executed by random groups of vengeful British soldiers, while the British administration looked the other way. Lord Canning, the British Viceroy, was concerned at this lawless behaviour of his own soldiers and complained to his superiors in London that "aged women and children are sacrificed as well as those guilty of rebellion."[10]

The brutality of the British soldiers was witnessed in Delhi the most. Having reconquered Delhi, which was temporarily taken over by Bahadur Shah during the revolt, the British had despatched Bahadur Shah to imprisonment in Burma (Myanmar) and unleashed a massacre on the Muslims in the city. Mirza Ghalib, renowned Muslim poet, was a witness to the developments in Delhi. In his personal diary, later published as *Dastanbuy* (Persian for bouquet), Ghalib lamented, "For you, this is only a sorrowful story, but the pain is so great that to hear it, the stars will weep tears of blood."[11]

Canning was not ready to be carried away by the vengeful mood of the British society. He firmly rejected the suggestions by irascible British officers to raze the Jama Masjid to ground. That invited derision from the British leaders, who ridiculed him as Clemency Canning. But Canning had a different wily idea. He advised his superiors in London that the only way to continue British Raj over the 150 million natives with the strength of a handful of officers and soldiers was to try and attenuate divisions within the Indian society in a subtle and unassuming manner. "If we destroy or desecrate Mussalman mosques or Brahmin temples, we do exactly what is wanting to band the two antagonist races against ourselves... As we must rule over 150 million of people by a handful (more or less small) of Englishmen, let us do it in the manner best calculated to leave them divided (as in religion and national feeling they already are) and to inspire them with the greatest possible awe of our power and with the least suspicion of our motives."[12]

Thus, the British had set in motion a plan to work towards destroying the unity and bonhomie witnessed among various sections of the Indian society in the 1857 revolt. Meanwhile, a section of the Muslims was so unnerved by the British oppression that it started questioning the wisdom of opposing the British and supporting Hindus.

* * *

Around the same time, certain developments in the Western world too had started influencing Indian Muslims once again. As modernity started influencing the Muslim lands in Europe and Arabia, a new revivalist movement took birth in mid-18th century. Started by a Sunni cleric and theologian, Muhammad Ibn Abd al-Wahhab, this puritanical, exclusivist and obscurantist Islamic movement, known today as Wahhabism, became a dominant stream in the Islamic world in the last two centuries. Heft was added to this brand of Islam when the new ruler of Arabia, Mohammad bin Saud, entered into an agreement with al-Wahhab in 1744 and made Wahhabism the state religion of the Saudi kingdom. Petro-dollars added further impetus to it in the 20th century. From Palestine to Pakistan, it is this hard-line Wahhabism that is leading to the rise of radicalism and fundamentalism among Muslims.

Wahhabism came to influence Indian Islam in the 18th century itself. Al-Wahhab's contemporary was a Delhi-based

Islamic theologian, called Shah Waliullah. Waliullah was very disturbed by the growing syncretic practices among the Muslims. He saw a big threat to Islam in the growing influence of Hindu customs and beliefs among the Muslims and decided to 'purify' Islam. Obsessed by the fear of 'danger to Islam', Waliullah even welcomed the invasion of India by the ruler of Afghanistan, Ahmed Shah Abdali.

Then came the Ahl-e-Hadith movement, started in Bhopal. This puritanical movement was also an attempt at negating the growing Hindu-Muslim bonhomie witnessed during the First War of Independence in 1857 and the syncretic Islam that was taking roots. That these revisionist and exclusivist movements by the fundamentalist preachers of Islam had succeeded in their mission can be gauged from the fact that the Hindus and Muslims who had fought together against the British in 1857, ended up fighting against each other nine decades later in 1947, resulting in the Partition of India on communal lines and the creation of Pakistan.

One glaring example of the success of Wahhabi ideology in India was the transformation witnessed in the eminent Muslim reformist and educationist of the 19th century, Sir Syed Ahmed Khan. Sir Syed is remembered for his contributions in the field of modern education for Muslims. He was the founder of Aligarh Muslim University, which was first started as the Mohammedan Anglo-Oriental College in 1875.

Sir Syed started off as a strong protagonist of Hindu-Muslim unity. He was friends with eminent Hindu leaders, like Swami Vivekananda and Devendranath Tagore. Addressing a large gathering in Gurdaspur on January 27,

1884, Sir Syed described Hindus and Muslims as one nation. "O Hindus and Muslims! Do you belong to a country other than India? Don't you live on the soil and are you not buried under it or cremated on its *ghats*? If you live and die on this land, then bear in mind that 'Hindu' and 'Muslim' is but religious word: all the Hindus, Muslims and Christians who live in this country are one nation," he proclaimed.

In fact, the First War of Independence in 1857 was fought against the British by Hindus and Muslims unitedly. After the war, the British came down heavily on the leadership of both the communities. The failure of the 1857 war and the subsequent brutality of the British had a different impact on some of the Muslim eminences, which included renowned Urdu poet Ghalib and an equally renowned Muslim educationist, Sir Syed Ahmed Khan. Both had firmly believed that it was a mistake on the part of the Muslims to join hands with the Hindus against the British.

Syed Ahmed, who had once proclaimed that everyone living in India, irrespective of his religion, was a Hindu, became a staunch critic of the 1857 war later. In a book he authored after the war, he described Muslims as the victims of war, rather than the willful perpetrators. He was in Bijnor at the time of the war. The Nawab of Bijnor was also participating in the war against the British. Syed Ahmed was busy arranging for the security of the British in Bijnor. He told the Nawab that "nobody can challenge the British sovereignty over India". After the war, Syed Ahmed took it upon himself to mobilise Muslim support for the British. He started an organization by the name, 'Loyal Mohammedans of India' and published stories of those Muslims who had helped protect the British officers and their families during the war. Talking of his efforts, Syed Ahmed, echoing

Macaulay's statement, had said that his aim was to create "a class of persons Mohammedan in religion, Indian in blood and colour, but English in tastes, in opinions, and in intellect."[13]

Syed Ahmed was also an ardent advocate of Urdu and went to the extent of calling Hindi as a "vulgar" language. This love of Urdu took him to the other extreme in his ideological beliefs. Two years after the famous Gurdaspur speech, Syed was heard at a speech in Meerut in 1886, openly articulating the theory that Muslims were a separate nation. "If we join the political movement of the Bengalis, our nation will reap a loss, for we do not want to become subjects of the Hindus instead of the subjects of the 'people of the Book...,'"[14] he argued, insisting that British rule was better than Hindu rule.

Further elaborating on this, Sir Syed openly advocated separate nationhood for Muslims. "Suppose that the English community and the army were to leave India, taking with them all their cannons and their splendid weapons and all else, who then would be the rulers of India?... Is it possible that under these circumstances, two nations – the Mohammedans and the Hindus – could sit on the same throne and remain equal in power? Most certainly not. It is necessary that one of them should conquer the other. To hope that both could remain equal is to desire the impossible and the inconceivable. But until one nation has conquered the other and made it obedient, peace cannot reign in the land," he insisted.[15]

"Oh, my brother Muslims! You have ruled over nations and have for centuries held different countries in your grasp. For seven hundred years in India, you had imperial sway. You know what it is to rule. The Bengalis had never at any period held sway over an inch of the Indian soil," Syed exclaimed. "We do not want to become the subjects of the Hindus instead of the people of the Book (Christians)," he declared.[16]

Thus, Syed Ahmed, who was championing Hindu-Muslim unity initially, became one of the earliest Muslim leaders to propagate that Muslims were a separate entity and they should be careful in protecting their separate identity from the Hindus. He also branded the Congress as a Hindu Bengali party. Hector Bolitho, the author of *Jinnah – Creator of Pakistan*, described Syed Ahmed as the first bold Indian Muslim to talk about Partition.

Thus, the first major articulation of the Two-Nation Theory was done by Syed Ahmed. It later became the foundational thesis for the Muslim League and was eventually used by Jinnah to partition India. Interestingly, Jinnah too started his political career as a champion as Hindu-Muslim unity before ending up as the Father of Pakistan. But Syed Ahmed must be credited with fathering the theory. "Pakistan is in reality the direct result of the whole scheme of things as envisaged by this good old man (Sir Syed), who represented in his person the ideology and aspirations of the whole Muslim nation of this sub-continent," wrote Pakistani scholars.[17]

* * *

The British had found this new development interesting and worth exploring for weakening the nationalist movement and perpetuation of their rule in India. Anglo-Mohammaden alliance, a project initiated by Syed Ahmed, became the new mantra for the British officers. Sir John Stratchey, a member of the Viceroy's Executive Council, suggested that the existence of "two hostile creeds" in India would benefit the British. He insisted that those Muslims would be the loyal pillars of the British Raj and "under no conceivable circumstances would (they) prefer Hindu domination to our own"[18]. They decided to put this discord between Hindus and Muslims to test by attempting a religious partition of the country.

First such partition of India was announced by the British in 1905. They decided to partition Bengal province into two. The capital of British India, until 1911, was Calcutta (today's Kolkata) in Bengal province. Bengal was the largest province in British India with over 80 million population in those days, almost one-fifth of the population of the entire country. It comprised of the present-day Bengal, Bangladesh, Bihar, Jharkhand, Assam and Orissa. Bengal was also home to a strong resistance movement against the British. A large number of revolutionaries in India's freedom movement came from Bengal. A strong Congress movement too flourished in the province. Poets, litterateurs, academics and journalists – Bengal was home to many eminences who were at the forefront of the struggle against the British.

The British had decided to tackle this fledgling anti-colonialist movement in a different way. They partitioned the province of Bengal into two – East Bengal with Dacca (present-day Dhaka) as the capital; that included Assam also, and West Bengal with Kolkata as the capital; that included Bihar and Orissa. Lord Curzon was the British Viceroy of India when Bengal was partitioned. Curzon argued that it was only an administrative measure. But his own colleagues, like Henry Cotton, the then Chief Commissioner of Assam, who was himself opposed to this move of Curzon, openly stated that the act was intended to weaken the nationalist movement in the region. "There were no administrative reasons. Curzon's plan was to oppress the rising force of a nationalist political movement," Henry Cotton wrote.

The Congress leadership and the revolutionaries smelt the mischief of the British behind this decision. Through this policy of *divide et impera* – divide and rule, the British had planned to secure two objectives. They wanted to weaken the freedom movement and sow the seeds of mistrust and conflict between the Hindus and Muslims in the process. The partitioned East Bengal was to become almost 60 per cent Muslim, while the residual West Bengal was to be 80 per cent Hindu. The leaders of the Independence movement had decided to firmly reject this British mischief.

Lord Curzon travelled across the length and breadth of the province. Everywhere he encountered popular resistance to his move. Even the Muslims, including the brother of the Nawab of Dacca, Khwaja Atiquallah were opposed to Bengal's Partition, but Curzon was adamant. He insisted that the Partition of Bengal was a 'settled fact' and October 16, 1905 was declared as the day of Partition. "The Bengalis, who like to think themselves a nation and who dream of a future when the English will have been turned out, and a Bengali Babu will be installed in the Government House, Calcutta, of course bitterly resent any disruption… If we are weak enough to yield to their clamour now, we shall not be able to dismember or reduce Bengal again; and you will be cementing and solidifying on the eastern flank of India a force already formidable, and certain to be a source of increasing trouble in future", he noted[19].

People were furious. Agitations, protests, lockdowns, speeches, writings and posters started dominating the province. On the appointed day of Partition, a massive protest rally was organised at Barisal town, in the then south-central Bengal, which is now in Bangladesh. Over fifty thousand people joined the protests. *Vande Mataram*, the song authored by Bankim Chandra Chattopadhyay, a Bengali scholar in his novel *Anandmath*, became the battle-cry of agitating masses – both Hindus and Muslims. Poet Rabindranath Tagore, one of the leading personalities of Bengal, equally respected by both communities in the province, was present to administer an oath to the people about the reunification of Bengal. At another big meeting in Calcutta on August 7, 1905, a resolution was passed which spoke about the need to boycott British products as long as "Partition resolution is not withdrawn". Thus was born the famous *swadeshi* movement.

The movement against the Partition of Bengal had soon spread to the whole country. The Indian National Congress was at the forefront. *Swaraj* and *swadeshi* became the twin *mantras* of the movement. It became popular as the *Vande Mataram* movement or the *swadeshi* movement. The national-level resistance was led by the trio popularly known as Lal-Bal-Pal – Lala Lajpat Rai in Punjab, Bal Gangadhar Tilak in Maharashtra and Bipin Chandra Pal in Bengal.

Although the movement began with the aim of undoing the Partition of Bengal, soon it became a movement against the British rule itself. Valentine Chirol, noted British journalist observed, "The question of Partition itself receded into background, and the issue, until then successfully veiled and now openly raised, was not whether Bengal should be an unpartitioned province or two-partitioned provinces under British rule, but whether the British rule itself was to endure in Bengal, for the matter of that, anywhere in India."[20]

The agitation became so intense that the British

Parliament was forced to take cognizance. Finally, the British emperor, King George V had to rush to India in December 1911 and declare the annulment of Bengal's Partition. Bengal became united again, unsettling Curzon's and his successor viceroy, Lord Minto's 'settled fact'. It was a great victory for the nationalist forces led by the Congress. But, by then, a large section of the Muslims of Bengal started seeing it as a defeat and were disheartened.

The resistance movement and its subsequent victory signified a major shift in the policies and programs of the Congress, which until then was a political body limited to filing complaints and petitions before the British administration. The *Vande Mataram* movement gave the radicals , led by Tilak, an upper hand in the Congress. The Congress now was transformed into a vehicle of popular resistance through public agitations. Tilak's historic exhortation– "Freedom is my birthright" – became the new *mantra* of Indian politics.

That was in 1905-11. A massive six-year nationwide agitation was launched when just one Indian province of Bengal was partitioned, and the British were forced to annul it. Fast forward to four decades. The entire country, including Bengal was partitioned and the same nation remained a mute witness. Why?

The answer lies in the history of the freedom movement during those fateful four decades. It is a tragic and revealing history, between 1905 and 1947, that has many startling facts and staggering lessons for India. What happened during those four decades must be revisited to understand those facts and learn those lessons.

* * *

The reaction of the Bengali Muslims to the Partition plan

was mixed. Muslims of East Bengal saw in it an opportunity to create a Muslim-majority province. A Muslim-owned paper in Calcutta, Mihir-O-Sudhakar, wrote on September 22, 1905, "The Muhammedan community should be thankful to the Government for the benefits which the Partition will confer on it"[21].

One of the critical fallouts of the Partition of Bengal was a meeting held at Dacca (Today's Dhaka) on December 27-31, 1906. The Ahsan Manzil, seat of the royal family, hosted the annual meeting of the Muhammadan Educational Conference. Nawab of Dacca, Khwaja Alimullah played host to over 3,000 delegates, who came from all over the country. Nawab Salimullah presented a proposal at the conference on December 30, for establishing a political party to safeguard the interests of Muslims in British India. The preparation for setting up a separate political party for Muslims had begun earlier that year at Lucknow and the Dacca Conference was the culmination of it.

Thus was born the All India Muslim League, with its headquarters at Lucknow. Renowned Shia cleric, Sir Aga Khan was elected as its first president. The objectives of the Muslim League were to create loyal Muslims to the British Raj and to advance the political rights of Muslims.

The British were excited at this development. The English press in India, largely controlled by the British went to town overplaying the birth of this new Muslim outfit. The Englishman wrote that the League would provide an effective answer to the Congress, while The Times of India reveled over the prospect of the League's "safe and sure rock of loyalty to the British Raj"[22].

The new Viceroy Lord Minto was also a happy man. "The

Muhammedan movement has done a great deal of good", he wrote to the British Emperor in December 1906. It clearly stated that "there are other factors to consider besides mere Bengali interests", he noted gleefully[23].

On the horizon of the Indian political firmament, a new player had emerged, with the tacit support and blessings of the British Viceroy, Lord Minto. This new player would change the future course of India's Independence movement in the next four decades substantively.

Reference—

1. *Durant, Will (1997): The Story of Civilisation, vol. I – Our Oriental Heritage, p. 1004-1005, Fine Communications, New York*
2. *Biruni, Muhammad bin Ahmad (1888): Al-Beruni's India: An Account of the Religion, Philosophy, Literature, Geography, Chronology, Astronomy, Customs, Laws and Astrology of India, p. 110, Trubner's Oriental Series*
3. *Biruni, Muhammad bin Ahmad (1888): Al-Beruni's India: An Account of the Religion, Philosophy, Literature, Geography, Chronology, Astronomy, Customs, Laws and Astrology of India, p. 22, Trubner's Oriental Series*
4. *Ibid*
5. *Sharma, Arvind: Hindu as a Missionary Religion,p. 15, State University of New York Press*
6. *Nanda, B.R.: Gandhi: Pan-Islamism, Imperialism and Nationalism, p. 7*
7. *Lane-Poole, Stanley (1908): Aurangzeb and the Decay of the Mughal Empire, p. 33, reproduced by Sani H. Panhwar*
8. *Savarkar, V.D. "The Indian War of Independence" 1857*
9. *The Times, August 12, 1857*
10. *Hansard's Parliamentary Debates: Third Series, Commencing with the Accession of William IV, Vol. CXLVIII, p. 906, Cornelius Buck*
11. *Mirza Asadullah Khan Ghalib, Dastanbuy: A Diary of the Indian Revolt of 1857, trans. Khwaja Ahmad Faruqi, p. 34, Asia Publishing House, Bombay*
12. *Hardy, P. (1973): The Muslims of British India, p. 72, Cambridge University Press*

13. *Lelyveld, David (1978): Aligarh's First Generation: Muslim Solidarity in British India, p. 207, Princeton University Press*
14. *Hardy, P (1973): The Muslims of British India, p. 130, Cambridge University Press*
15. *Hiro, Dilip (2015): The Longest August: The Unflinching Rivalry between India and Pakistan, p. 19, Nation Books*
16. *Ahmed, Sir Syed (1888): On the Present State of Indian Politics, p. 50-51, Pioneer Press, Allahabad*
17. *Dar, Bashir Ahmed (1971): Religious Thought of Sayyid Ahmad Khan, p. vi, The University of Michigan*
18. *Das, M.N. "Indian National Congress vs. the British" pp. 275, Ajanta Publishers, 1978*
19. *Nanda, B.R. (1989), "Gandhi: Pan-Islamism, Imperialism and Nationalism In India" pp. 65, Oxford University Press, Delhi*
20. *Chirol, Valentine (1910): Indian Unrest, p. 88, Macmillan and Co. Limited*
21. *Nanda, B.R. (1989), "Gandhi: Pan-Islamism, Imperialism and Nationalism In India" pp. 65, Oxford University Press, Delhi*
22. *Nanda, B.R. (2015), "Gokhale: The Indian Moderates and the British raj" pp. 336, Princeton University Press*
23. *Nanda, B.R. (1989), "Gandhi: Pan-Islamism, Imperialism and Nationalism In India" pp. 74, Oxford University Press, Delhi*

□

Without Hindu Muslim Unity No Freedom

Hindus, if they want unity among different races, must have the courage to trust the minorities.

—Gandhi

Muslim League's leadership, including Aga Khan, was clear from the beginning that they needed to win the goodwill of the British Government in order to secure maximum concessions from them. They also established a Muslim League branch in London and started cultivating a group of parliamentarians in the British Parliament for their support.

Meanwhile, the Vande Mataram movement started picking up momentum in the country. What the British thought would be a movement of the Bengali Bhadralok became a pan-Indian movement. The British noticed it and decided to work on the demand of the Congress Moderates regarding introducing direct elections and increasing the participation of Indians in the Central and provincial governments. The Muslim League was fearful of the Congress' demand for self-rule, which it imagined as the Hindu rule, and decided to demand separate representation for the Muslims. It immediately swung into action and a delegation led by Sir Aga Khan approached Viceroy and Governor-General Lord Minto in Shimla on October 1, 1906. Their central demand was for separate electorates for Muslims at all levels of government, including legislative councils, district boards and municipalities. The League leadership argued for exclusive Muslim seats, greater in proportion to their numerical strength, "in view of 'the value of the contribution' Muslims were making as rulers earlier for a long period, and 'to the defence of the empire'."

Under the Act of 1892 in the United Province, where the Muslims were fourteen percent of the population, they had not secured a single seat by joint franchise. If they wanted to get any seats, they had to join hands with the Hindus and thus forfeit their own interests. So, they insisted that Muslims should be given separate representation for both local bodies and legislative councils, through separate electorates. The viceroy listened to them and promised them that their demands would be forwarded to the British Government. Encouraged by this positive response from the British officials, Muslim leadership went ahead and established their own political party – the All India Muslim League in December 1906.

Although Lord Minto, who succeeded Lord Curzon as the Viceroy, was sympathetic to the demands of the Muslim League and assured support to them, Secretary Morley was not convinced about creating exclusive electorates and instead proposed mixed electorates. It led to protracted negotiations in London. The League leadership vociferously protested, calling it a 'betrayal'. Morley was in favour of acceding to the demand of the Congress Moderates in granting limited self-rule, so that the nationalist fervor building across the country through the *Vande Mataram* movement could be diffused. But the League leadership had enlisted the support of some British parliamentarians, forcing Secretary Morley to finally climb down and announce in the House of Lords on February 23, 1909 that he was conceding the demand of the League for separate electorates.

"The Muhammedans demand the election of their own representatives on these Councils in all the stages... Secondly, they want a number of seats somewhat in excess of their numerical strength", Secretary Morley told the Parliament, adding "These two demands we are quite ready and intend to meet in full"[1]. A new phrase "weighted representation" was born and the League would continue to harp on the principle afterwards in place of "proportional representation".

It was the first major victory for the nascent League; but it decided to increase the bargain. Expressing unhappiness over the number of seats allocated to the Muslims, the League continued its agitation. The London branch of the League got into action and mobilised support from several parliamentarians. Fearing that the Indian Councils Bill, granting elected representation to Indians in the imperial legislatures, would not be passed in the British Parliament without securing League's support, the British leadership blinked. Finally, an agreement was reached between the League leadership and the Minto-Morley duo in September 1909.

It was a massive morale booster for the newly formed Muslim League. Although claimed to represent the Muslim community, it still didn't have any massive support of the community. But the Minto-Morley Reforms provided the right launch pad for its growth. But the tragedy was that those reforms had 'legalized communalism'. Thus, Minto-

Morley became fathers of communal electorates in India, a legacy that ended finally in the Partition of the country.

As for the Moderates in the Congress, what they demanded was self-rule but what they got was 'benevolent despotism'.

* * *

Emergence of Muslim League on the political horizon and the open patronage that the British extended to it came as a challenge to the Congress. Until then, the Congress projected itself as the collective voice of all Indians. Earlier efforts to create a rift between Hindus and Muslims and to distance Muslims from the freedom struggle did not succeed much. After the formation of the Indian National Congress in 1885, a section of the Muslims too joined it and started working with other Hindu leaders. But leaders like Syed Ahmed Khan, with full support of the British, continued their efforts to wean away the Muslims from the Congress' integrationist platform.

Badruddin Tyabji, a renowned Muslim lawyer from Bombay and his elder brother Camruddin became active members of the Congress during the initial years. Badruddin even became the president of the Congress in 1887-88. Responding to the scepticism induced both by the British and leaders like Syed Ahmed in the Muslims about participation in Congress activity, Tyabji categorically declared, "I, at least, not merely in my individual capacity but as representing the Anjuman-i-Islam of Bombay, do not consider that there is anything whatever in the position or the relations of the different communities of India – be they Hindus, Musalmans, Parsis, or Christians – which should induce the leaders of any one community to stand aloof from the others in their efforts to obtain those great general reforms, those great general rights, which are for the common benefit of us all."[2]

The Congress continued to attract people from all communities, but the rise of the Muslim League as a political entity in 1906 altered that situation. After the 1857 revolt, the next big challenge that the British faced was from the *Vande Mataram* or *swadeshi* movement. It began as a local movement for unification of Bengal, but soon became a pan-Indian movement for uprooting the British Empire. The rattled British resorted to the trick of divide and rule. They focused on Muslims of Bengal for support. Khwaja Salimullah, the Nawab of Bengal was co-opted by offering a massive amount of 1.4 million rupees. Salimullah joined the Muslim League and became its vice president.

With the blessings of the British, the League began an aggressive campaign with serious communal overtones. A pamphlet called *Lal Ishtar* – Red Pamphlet - was distributed at the Dacca session of the League in 1906. One of Salimullah's cronies, Ibrahim Khan was the author of this pamphlet. The pamphlet contained the following highly provocative material:

- The Hindus, by various stratagems, are relieving the Mahomedans of nearly the whole of the money earned by them. Among the causes of the degradation of Mahomedans is their association with the Hindus.
- Among the means to be adopted for the amelioration of Mahomedans, is boycotting Hindus.
- O' Musalmans! Arise, awake! Do not read in the same schools with Hindus. Do not buy anything from a Hindu shop. Do not touch any article manufactured by Hindu hand. Do not give any employment to a Hindu.

Do not accept any degrading office under a Hindu. You are ignorant, but if you acquire knowledge, you can at once send all Hindus to *jehannum* (hell). You form the majority of the population of this province. Among the cultivators alsoyou form the majority. It is agriculture that is the source of wealth. The Hindu has no wealth of his own and has made himself rich only by despoiling you or your wealth. If you become sufficiently enlightened, then the Hindus wall starve and soon become Mahomedans.

- Hindus are very selfish. As the progress of Mahomedans is inimical to the self-aggrandisement of Hindus, the latter will always oppose Mahomedan progress for their selfish ends.
- Be united in boycotting Hindus. What dire mischief have they not done to us! They have robbed us of honour and wealth. They have deprived us of our daily bread. And now they are going to deprive us of our very life.[3]

The British and the League had the same agenda–weakening the Congress-led national movement against the British Raj. Communal tensions started rising. East Bengal witnessed widespread riots and violence in 1907 in which Hindus became victims of both rioters and the rulers. The Bengal Nawab was seen openly instigating Muslim mobs while the British lent their helping hand to him.

The British war correspondent, H.W. Nevinson, who visited India during that period, narrated the following account in his 1908 book, *The New Spirit in India*:

"I have almost invariably found English officers on the side of the Mohammedan, where there is any rivalry of religion in East Bengal. This national inclination is now encouraged by the government's open resolve to retain the Mohammedan support of the Partition by any means. It was against the Hindus only that all the petty persecution of officialdom was directed. It was they who were excluded from government posts; it was Hindu schools from which government patronage was withdrawn. When Mohammedans rioted, the punitive police ransacked Hindu houses. *Mullahs* went through the country, preaching the revival of Islam and proclaiming to the villagers that the British Government was on the Mohammedan side, that the law courts had been specially suspended for three months, and no penalty would be exacted for violence done to Hindus, or for the loot of Hindu shops, or the abduction of Hindu widows. A *Red Pamphlet* was everywhere circulated, maintaining the same wild doctrines. In Comilla, Jamalpur and a few other places, rather serious riots occurred – lives were lost, temples were desecrated, images broken, shops plundered, and many Hindu widows carried off. Some of the towns were deserted, the Hindu population took refuge in '*pucca*' houses (i.e. house with brick in stone walls), women spent nights hidden in tanks, the crime known as 'group-rape' increased, and throughout the country districts there reigned a general terror, which still prevailed at the time of my visit."[4]

* * *

Provisions of the Minto-Morley Reforms brought further deterioration in the situation. They went beyond electoral arena into administrative and governance issues. Their discriminatory character had greatly distressed the stalwart among the Congress Moderates – Gopal Krishna Gokhale, who called the reforms as "discouraging to all communities except the Muslims". Writing to his son Jawaharlal in March 1909, Motilal Nehru said that the reforms had further exacerbated Hindu-Muslim antagonism, and "our Anglo-Indian friends have distinctly scored in this matter, and no amount of council reform will repair the mischief."

The Minto-Morley Reforms came as a shock to the Congress leadership. They realised that the British were luring away Muslims through concessions, like separate electorates. It was a new and unexpected challenge for the elite Congress leadership. Pandit Madan Mohan Malviya, in his presidential address to the Indian National Congress session at Lahore in 1909, expressed disappointment over these reforms, saying, "We find that the regulations have been vitiated by the disproportionate representation which they have secured to Mohammadans and to the landed classes, and the small room for representation which they have left for the educated classes, also by the fact that they have made an invidious and irritating distinction between Muslim and non-Muslim subjects of His Majesty, in the matter of the protection of minorities and franchise and lastly in that, they have laid down unnecessarily narrow and arbitrary restrictions in the choice of the electors".[5]

There was one Hindu leader though, who took a different approach at that time. He was not in the Congress yet, and not even in India. But he took interest in Indian politics from a distance in South Africa through his mentor and political *guru*, Gopal Krishna Gokhale. That leader was Mohandas Karamchand Gandhi, who became the unquestioned king of the Congress movement a decade later. Gandhi lived in Transvaal in South Africa at that time. He led a joint struggle of all coloured people against British oppression. Gandhi was in London when the Minto-Morley Reforms were formally announced. Separate electorates, weightage disproportionate to population of the Muslims and other discriminatory aspects of the reforms didn't disconcert Gandhi. Instead, he suggested that the Hindus "should cheerfully concede to their Muslim brethren the utmost they can".[6]

Instead of standing firm against these dangerously communal and divisive provisions, the Moderate Congress leadership decided to opt for the Gandhian remedy – a less arduous path of appeasing the Muslim leadership in the country. Something must be done to keep the Muslims on the side of the Congress. The Moderate leaders like Gokhale started making moves. As a first step, the Congress, which had earlier opposed the move, almost accepted the communal electorates under Minto-Morley Reforms in December 1911 at the AICC session at Bankipore, in Bihar. This was Congress' first major surrender before the communal League leadership. Congress' stand was that it neither supported nor rejected separate electorates. When Pandit Madan Mohan Malviya, the senior Congress leader, brought forward a resolution in the Imperial Legislative Council seeking a review of the excess representation for the Muslims in the new legislatures, there was nobody to support him. The Hindu members of the Congress too were unhappy that Malviya was raking up an unnecessary controversy.

Although Minto-Morley Reforms brought cheers to the Muslim League leadership and the Muslim community supporting it, they were soon heartbroken and angry over the British decision to annul the Bengal Partition in 1911. Partition of Bengal into East and West, by which East Bengal became predominantly Muslim was supported by a large number of Muslims in the region. The Nawab of Bengal himself supported it, though his stepbrother Khwaja Atiquallah not only opposed the Partition actively, but also brought a resolution against it at the Calcutta session of the Congress in 1906. But his opposition was more to do with the animosity he had for his brother Salimullah than about Hindu-Muslim unity.

When Viceroy Curzon announced the Partition plan in 1904, the immediate response of the Muslims was negative. But Curzon made special efforts to convince them by undertaking a tour of East Bengal. He went to Mymensingh, Chittagong and Dacca and addressed Muslim groups. He explained to them that under his scheme, the entire Assam Commissionerate would be given to East Bengal in addition to existing fifteen districts. This would make it a big province with 31 million population, majority of whom will be Muslims. Curzon's plan was to include Tripura Hills, Assam and Chittagong, Dacca, Rajshahi and Malda regions into the new province of East Bengal.

In his address at Dacca on February 18, 1904, Curzon hinted that Dacca could become the capital of East Bengal. Calling their culture 'superior', Curzon tried to entice the Muslims by saying that "the people of these districts (which were to become East Bengal), by reason of their numerical strength and their superior culture, the preponderating voice in the province so created, which would invest the Mohammedans in Eastern Bengal with a unity, which they have since the days of the old Mussalman Viceroys and kings".[7]

Curzon's efforts led to the Bengali Muslim *bhadralok* discovering that the Partition of Bengal was an attractive proposition and they supported it. Soon the ordinary Muslim masses too joined them. "Except for a handful, like Barrister Abdul Rasul, the majority of the Muslims in East Bengal supported Partition and viewed the anti-partition agitation as an attempt to deny them an opportunity to have a Muslim-majority province," writes Nitish Sengupta in his book, *Bengal: The Unmaking of a Nation*.[8]

Therefore, when the Royal Proclamation for Partition of Bengal was announced on October 16, 1905, the province witnessed two distinctly opposite reactions. While the mainstream Bengali society, including some prominent Muslims, erupted in anger, the majority of Muslims cheered in joy. "People of Calcutta observed it as the day of mourning," wrote *Amrita Bazar Patrika* of Calcutta in its editorial on the next day.[9] Gurudev Rabindranath Tagore expressed his anguish through a popular poem: "*Banglar mati, Banglar jal, Banglar bayu, Banglar phal, punya houk, hey Bhagaban...*" (May the soil, water, air and fruits be hallowed). He himself led the protest march of more than fifty thousand people, tying *rakhi* to each other and symbolising brotherhood of all Bengalis. '*Amar Shonar Bangla*' became the war-song of the masses. After taking the holy bath in River Ganges, Tagore imparted a pledge to them that they shall reunite Bengal.

On the other hand, Nawab Salimullah started Mohammedan Provincial Union in October 1905 with a view to mobilising Muslims of East and West Bengal in support of the Partition. Soon the Muslim masses started seeing Partition as a beneficial arrangement for them and started organising rallies, urging their co-religionists to remain faithful to the government. This led to tensions between the communities culminating in communal clashes throughout 1906-07. While Viceroy Curzon was denounced by Hindus in particular, and anti-partitionists in general, the newly appointed Lt. Governor of East Bengal, Bampfylde Fuller received a rousing reception from the Muslims of Dacca.

The intensity of the *Vande Mataram* movement had finally forced the British Government and King George V, who came to Delhi for his Coronation Durbar in December 1911, to announce the revocation of the Partition of Bengal, which was to formally come into effect from April 1, 1912. To placate the Muslims, he also announced that the capital of British India would be shifted from the Hindu-majority Calcutta to Muslim-majority Delhi. A new university and high court were also granted to Dacca.

But the British decision of annulment of Partition came as a shock to the Muslims of Bengal. They felt betrayed by the regime and agitated over the Congress' opposition, which they saw as Hindu opposition. While Minto-Morley Reforms proved a morale booster to Muslim separatism, annulment of Bengal Partition threw cold water on their spirits and rekindled the hopes for national unity in the minds of some Congress leaders.

* * *

Congress and other nationalist forces had succeeded in annulling Bengal's Partition. But the British had succeeded in destroying Hindu-Muslim cohesion and in germinating the worm of separatism in the minds of the Indian Muslims. Majority of them saw the annulment as a Hindu victory. Maulana Mohammad Ali, president of the League at that time and who would become the president of the Congress itself a decade later, called the British decision a "great blunder". He warned Hindus not to be arrogant and "carried away by a feeling of triumph".

The British used Minto-Morley Reforms as a carrot to attract the Muslims. As demanded, Muslims were granted disproportionately higher representation in the Imperial and provincial legislative councils to their population. Separate electorates, where only Muslims could vote, were created. Muslims were granted voting rights more liberally than their non-Muslim counterparts. All this resulted in fortifying a sense of separateness in the minds of the Indian Muslims, which the subsequent leadership of the Muslim League would exploit.

Although succeeded in ending Bengal's Partition through a sustained nationwide agitation for six years, the Congress started believing that winning over the Muslim support was crucial for its future campaign of freedom. As a first step, the Moderates in Congress wanted to win over the Muslim League leadership. League's president Aga Khan was in London at that time. Moderate Congress leader, Gopal Krishna Gokhale and his disciple at that time, who would later become the architect of Muslim separatism in India, Mohammad Ali Jinnah, too were in London. Gokhale and Jinnah approached Aga Khan with a proposal that he should preside over the Congress session at Bankipur near Patna in Bihar, in 1912. Aga Khan's separatist and pro-British views were well-known . Yet, in their eagerness to win over Muslims by hook or by crook, the Congress leadership decided to turn a blind eye to all that.

Aga Khan rejected the proposal, but the new attitude in the Congress leadership, that "without Hindu-Muslim unity, no freedom", was further consolidated. Thereafter, it was simply a race between the two parties – the Congress and the British – to allure the League. On its part, the League would always side with the highest bidder, which was the

British, most of the time.

This phase of the Independence movement gave birth to the most controversial leader of the times, a leader who was initially hailed as the 'Ambassador of Hindu-Muslim unity', but who ended up becoming the 'Father of Pakistan', Mohammad Ali Jinnah.

The Independence movement was never the same again.

Reference—

1. *Morley, Viscount (2012) "Indian Speeches" pp. 126, Createspeace Independent Publisher,*
2. *Zaidi, A.M. (1985), "Congress Presidential Addresses Volume One: 1885-1900" Indian Institute of Applied Political Research, New Delhi; Noorani, A.G. (1969), "Builders of Modern India: Badruddin Tyabji" p. 60, Publications Division, Ministry of Information and Broadcasting, Government of India*
3. *Balakrishna, Sandeep (2019), "The Lal Ishtar and the Bloodbath of Hindus in Bengal" The Dharma Dispatch accessed at https://www.dharmadispatch.in/history/the-lal-ishtahar-and-the-bloodbath-of-hindus-in-bengal*
4. *Nevinson, H.W. (1908), "The New Spirit in India" p. 202, Harper and Brothers*
5. *Ed. Banerjee, A.C. (1945), "Indian Constitutional Documents" Vol. III, p. 269-270, Calcutta, India*
6. *Gandhi, Mahatma, "The Collected Works of Mahatma Gandhi" Vol. 9; July 23, 1908 – August 4, 1909, Gandhi Sevagram Ashram, https://www.gandhiashramsevagram.org/gandhi-literature/mahatma-gandhi-collected-works-volume-9.pdf p. 265*
7. *"Speeches By Lord Curzon of Kedleston, Viceroy and Governor General of India" Vol. III, 1902-1905, p. 302-303, Office of the Superintendent of Government Printing, India*
8. *Sengupta, Nitish (2007), "Bengal Divided: The Unmaking of a Nation" p. 16-17, Random House Publishers India Pvt. Ltd.*
9. *Amrita Bazar Patrika, October 17, 1905*

□

The Ambassador of Hindu – Muslim Unity

Few individuals significantly alter the course of history. Fewer still modify the map of the world. Hardly anyone can be credited with creating a nation-state. Jinnah did all the three.

—Stanley Wolpert

In an effort to win over the Muslim League, Moderate Congress leaders had decided to use Mohammad Ali Jinnah, a London-graduated barrister and an associate of Gokhale. Jinnah, like Gandhi and Nehru, attended the same league of colleges in London, although in different years. Jinnah returned to India in 1896. He formally joined the Indian National Congress in 1906, the same year when the Muslim League was born. He was among the 44 Muslim delegates attending that session of 1500 Congress delegates. He became the secretary of a Congress stalwart, Dadabhai Naoroji.

Jinnah, being a Muslim in an organisation predominantly Hindu, received special attention in the Congress. He also made right noises on several occasions. He opposed the partition of Bengal, describing it as "the obnoxious virus introduced into the body politic of India with evil design". When the Aga

Khan delegation met Viceroy Minto in Shimla in 1906, Jinnah demanded to know what right "these gentlemen possessed" to speak for Bombay. Who had elected them? He opposed the provision of separate electorates under the Minto-Morley reforms in 1909, arguing that they reduced Indian politics into two "watertight compartments"[1]. In 1913, he even told the Islington Committee on administrative reforms that "I do not see why a Hindu should not be in charge of a district where the majority happens to be Mohammedan"[2]. Leaders like Sarojini Naidu even gave him the epithet of the 'Ambassador of Hindu-Muslim unity'. He was and continued to be considered a secular and non-practicing Muslim. Non-practicing, he was, but was he secular? Facts speak otherwise.

One of the best portrayals of Jinnah was done by Ayesha Jalal, a Pakistani professor, who teaches at the Tufts University in the US, in her book, *The Sole Spokesman*. Jinnah always wanted to be the 'sole spokesman'[3] for Indian Muslims, whether inside the Congress or subsequently as the leader of the Muslim League. As long as he was hailed by the Congress leaders as the 'Ambassador of Hindu-Muslim unity' and assigned important tasks, like midwifing with the League, he was happily a Congressman and a nationalist. But when Gandhi started cultivating other Muslim Leaders, Jinnah felt that his one-upmanship was ending and quit the Congress.

As mentioned earlier, he was the go-between for Congress to cultivate leaders of the League. He was there when Congress tried to unsuccessfully woo Aga Khan. Afterwards, he formally joined the Muslim League in 1913 with the mission of bringing it closer to the Congress in the Independence movement. He played an important role in bringing Congress and League on one platform at Lucknow in December 1916. But when the Gandhi era began in Congress after 1918, and Gandhi started cultivating other Muslim leaders, like Maulana Mohammad Ali and Shaukat Ali, Jinnah was disturbed. Blaming Gandhi for promoting those leaders, Jinnah left the Congress in 1920 and joined the League.

As for his secularism, although he never appeared to be visiting mosques, etc., he nevertheless held Islamist identity all-through. The maiden intervention he made in the 22nd session of Congress at Calcutta in 1906, was in support of a resolution brought by two Muslim members. "It is a matter of gratification to the whole Muhammadan community that we have got on the programme of the Indian National Congress a question which purely affects the Muhammadan community. That shows one thing, gentlemen, that we Muhammadans can equally stand on this common platform and pray for our grievances being remedied through the programme of the National Congress," he told his community through that platform.[4]

When separate electorates for Muslims were announced under Minto-Morley reforms, Jinnah was one of the first to get into the Imperial Legislature. He was instrumental in bringing the Muslim League to the Congress and clinching a communal deal in favour of the League in the name of the Lucknow Pact, in 1916. He continued his dual membership in Congress and League for seven years before finally quitting Congress for good, in 1920. Although his apologists blamed Gandhi for Jinnah leaving the Congress and credited him with taking a principled stand against Khilafat by leaving Congress, Jinnah himself gave a different logic. He told his journalist friend, Durga Das, that there was no place for him in Gandhi's Congress. "Gandhi worships the cow, and I eat it," Jinnah said, an argument he later repeated in many public speeches.[5]

An ardent supporter of Jinnah's politics, A.G. Noorani, in an article in the *Frontline* magazine, quotes Ian Bryant Wells, an Australian scholar, who wrote of Jinnah's shrewdness, "As a Muslim with a demonstrated record of concern for Muslim community, he was in a position to pressurise the Muslims to reduce their demands without being seen as a Congress lackey. As a noted nationalist and a colleague of Gokhale, he was similarly able to persuade the Hindus to make concessions to the Muslims without being labelled a communalist".[6] That was probably why eminent Left historian, Bipin Chandra described Jinnah as a "communal nationalist".

"Jinnah was committed to ends without great regard to means. His 'end' was always the protection of the Muslim community, but his chosen means changed as British India was dismantled. Initially, he placed his trust in electoral safeguards and weighted representative bodies; later, in separatism", writes British author Roderick Matthews, and adds "At no point after 1909 did Jinnah not represent Muslims and he never abandoned his obligations to them"[7].

* * *

Jinnah worked on the League leadership to join hands with the Congress and opposed the British. Although benefitted by the Minto-Morley reforms, the League leadership was annoyed with the British for annulling Bengal's Partition.

A new development in Europe around that time also pushed the Indian Muslims away from the British. In

September 1911, Italy attacked Tripoli, then a province of the Ottoman Turkish Empire. Several European countries, like Greece, Bulgaria and Serbia, joined hands with Italy. Even Russia supported it while the other major Western powers remained neutral. This had angered Muslims in Arab lands, for whom, the Khalifa of the Ottoman Empire was the leader of the entire Muslim Ummah. Indian Muslims too saw in it a Western effort to weaken Islamic Turkey. Neutrality of Great Britain was seen by the Indian Muslims as tacit support to Italy. They saw in it not just a clash within Europe, but a clash between the Cross and the Crescent.

As a retaliatory measure, they thought of drawing closer to the Congress. They thought it to be a better bargain for putting pressure on the British too. Valentine Chirol, a celebrated journalist from *The Times*, London, wrote to Viceroy Hardinge on December 22, 1912, cautioning about the same. "I had an interesting talk with Aga Khan. He says we seem to underrate the intensity of the anti-English feeling, which our failure to help Turkey, coming on top of Morocco, Tripoli and Persia has engendered. For the moment, at any rate, instead of convincing the Indian Muhammedans that they must more and more turn to the Raj for their protection, it is driving them to join hands with the Hindu politicians in revolt – not active, but political – against the Raj," he wrote.[8]

That period between 1911 and 1916 also witnessed the rise of the politics of *ummah* and pan-Islamism in India. Many prominent Muslim leaders with pan-Islamist credentials started emerging on the political horizon. Prominent among them were eminent scholars like Ameer Ali and poet Mohammad Iqbal. Ameer Ali, in his book, *The Spirit of Islam*, glorified the good old days of Islam and expressed dismay and dissent about the present. He claimed that the real history of India began only with the advent of Islam in the country.

Mohammad Iqbal, one of the architects of Pakistan, too emerged on the scene, promoting the idea of Islamic nationhood. In an article published in the *Hindustan Review* in August 1909, Iqbal questioned the very idea of a nation state, saying, "The expression Indian Muhammadan, however convenient it may be, is a contradiction in terms, since Islam in its essence is above all conditions of time and space. Nationality with us is a pure idea; it has no geographical basis. But inasmuch as the average man demands a material centre of nationality, the Muslim looks for it in the holy town of Mecca".[9]

The famous Ali Brothers, who became close friends of Gandhi during the Khilafat movement, too belonged to the same category. Mohammad Ali and Shaukat Ali hailed from the Muslim-majority town of Rampur in Western Uttar Pradesh. Mohammad Ali started his career as a journalist, but soon rose in the ranks of the Muslim League to become its president. During the Khilafat movement, Mohammad Ali became a close associate of Gandhi and even presided over the Congress session at Kakinada, in 1923.

Mohammad Ali was a firm believer in the separate identity of Hindus and Muslims. As a staunch supporter of Bengal's Partition, he even questioned the very idea of Indian national identity. In a letter written to Gokhale, in February 1908, he strongly resented Congress' opposition to Bengal's Partition. "To talk of unity in this connection is absurd," he angrily wrote, adding, "I know how territorialism appeals to Hindu mind. But it is unfair to demand the same intensity and fervour from Mosalmans who are and have been for 13 centuries 'a nation without a country'. We should be pardoned if we refuse to believe in the honesty of the declaration of unity of men, like Mr. Tilak, Mr. Dutt and Mr. Madan Mohan Malviya."[10]

Chaudhary Khaliquzzaman, a senior League leader, in his autobiography reveals stunning facts about the Ali Brothers who Gandhi trusted with his life. Shaukat Ali sent five thousand rupees to one Obeidullah Sindhi for organizing revolutionary activity abroad, and for inciting the Afghan Nawab to attack the British in India, he wrote. He also claimed that he was personally present at a meeting in the Ali Brothers' house in Chhindwara when Mohammad Ali passed a message to the German High Command through a German internee with the advise "to shift the theatre of war from the west to the east" and to attack India; he undertook to lead the revolt against the British from "somewhere in Bhopal", as soon as the German armies started advancing on India[11].

Such was the character of Mohammad Ali, who would later call "a fallen Muslim to be better than Gandhi"[12], whom all the senior Congress leaders, including Tilak and Anne Besant, came to support. Gandhi's support was inexplicable. He hardly knew the Ali Brothers when he went out of his way and demonstrated a tenacity that was undeserving for their release from jail in 1918. "Why should the Ali Brothers be in jail and why I remain outside", he bemoaned.

Another Muslim leader, who remained a Congress leader till the end, needs a special mention here. Maulana Abul Kalam Azad, born in Mecca to a Sufi father, also belonged to the same creed of Muslim leaders during the pre-Khilafat years as he advocated pan-Islamism. As a young journalist, Azad, which incidentally was his chosen pen name, won accolades for his writing skills and clarity of thoughts. Azad began his journalistic career in 1912 with an Urdu journal by name *Al Hilal*. "The fundamental mission of *Al Hilal* is to invite the Muslims to follow only the book of God and the traditions of the Prophet in all their activities and beliefs. Be it the field of education, culture or politics, it is subject to religion. The *Al Hilal* wants to see Mussalmans only as Mussalmans. We have learnt all our politics from religion. We believe that every idea which is derived from any source other than the Quran is patent heresy, and this applies to politics also," he wrote in an editorial.[13]

Responding to a question as to which political party should the Muslims join, Azad grandiloquently replied: "Mussalmans need not join any party. They are the ones who for centuries made the world join their party and follow their path. They constitute the party of God. As in other things, so in politics, the *Al Hilal* calls upon you never to put undue trust in government nor to take lessons from Hindus".[14]

Taking his beliefs forward, he even established a party called Jamait-i-Hizbullah (The Party of God), although it never took off. Not to leave his colleagues in the Congress in any doubt, Azad categorically stated as late as in 1940, while presiding over the Ramgarh session of the Congress, "I stand where I did in my early years in 1912".[15]

It was with such Muslim leaders that the Congress had attempted an alliance in order to secure Independence.

* * *

Congress and Muslim League held their session at Bombay in 1915 almost at the same time. The Congress constituted a committee to persuade the League to agree for a joint session. Jinnah was also there, as a member of both the parties. The League leadership did not agree. Surendranath

Banerjee, the Congress president that year, sent a message of 'affectionate greetings' to the League leadership on the day of their session. No reciprocal message came. In fact, the Bombay session of the League was a stormy affair. Jinnah was playing a key role in its proceedings, which the hardline leaders didn't quite appreciate. They saw him as a Congress stooge and started opposing his efforts to bring League closer to Congress vociferously. Matters reached a peak when some hooligans hired by the hardline Muslim leaders vandalized the League venue forcing Jinnah and others to flee to Taj Mahal Hotel for rest of the proceedings of the session.

However, Raja of Mohammadabad and Jinnah continued their efforts for Hindu-Muslim entente. Jinnah, just three years into the League, was elected the President for its session in 1916. He ensured that the League agreed to join the Congress session at Lucknow. Thus began a new chapter in Hindu-Muslim relations. Although short-lived, this experiment helped the Congress leadership realise the communalist and fundamentalist nature of the League. It is another matter that the Congress never took any strong position against it, because, by then, it became a conviction with the Congress leadership that "without Hindu-Muslim unity, no freedom."

The Muslim League had joined the Congress session at Lucknow in December 29-31, 1916 on the condition that the Congress would not oppose separate Muslim electorates in the provincial legislatures. The Congress, which initially opposed, then remained neutral to the demand of 'weighted representation' of Muslims, finally conceded the principle in the joint declaration.

The famous Lucknow Pact of 1916, that paved the way for the Congress and the League to come together, was thus a bargain struck between the two sides.

Through the Lucknow Pact, the League succeeded in forcing the Congress to formally agree to separate electorates, communal weightage and one-third representation for Muslims in legislatures. While the Congress, and later Indian historians, described the Pact as a great victory for Hindu-Muslim unity, it was described by later-day Pakistani commentators as the first major milestone for Pakistan. The acceptance of Congress for separate electorates was interpreted by them as its acknowledgement of the 'Two-Nation Theory'.

Much later, in 1936, Jinnah asked the same question: "When the Hindus accepted a separate identity for Muslims through the Lucknow Pact in 1916, how can they now object to Pakistan?"[16]

Covered under the title, 'Scheme of Reforms passed at the 31st Session of the Indian National Congress held at Lucknow on December 29, 1916 and adopted by the All-India Moslem League at its Meeting on December 31, 1916', the Lucknow Pact practically conceded all the separatist demands of the League.

- On the League demand of separate electorates, Congress agreed to end its ambiguity and supported them.
- Muslims were given one-third representation in the Imperial Legislative Council. A weightage formula was accepted by which Muslims were given more seats than their population would have allowed.
- The Muslims shall be elected through special

electorates and their strength in the different provinces shall be: 50% in Punjab where their population was 55%; 40% in Bengal where their population was 52%; 30% in U.P. where their population was mere 14%; 25% in Bihar where their population was mere 13%; 15% in C.P. where their population was 10%; and 33% in Bombay where they were 20%.

- No bill, nor any clause thereof, nor a resolution introduced by a non-official member effecting one or other community shall be presented in the assembly without approval of the concerned group.

"Our constitutional battle may be said to have been half won already," Jinnah declared jubilantly in his presidential address to the All-India Muslim League.[17] It may be worth mentioning here that it was the same Jinnah, who had proposed an amendment to the resolution in the 1906 Congress session at Calcutta on 'Self-government and *Swadeshi'*, in which he said that "there is in this resolution a mention that there should be a reservation for the backwardly educated classes. If the Mohamedan community is meant by it, I wish to draw your attention to the fact that the Mohamedan community should be treated in the same way as the Hindu community. The foundation upon which the Indian National Congress is based is that we are all equal, that there should be no reservation for any class or any community and my whole object is that reservation should be deleted".[18] Just a decade later, he gleefully championed the same.

Overnight, senior Congress leaders like Bal Gangadhar Tilak, Surendranath Banerjea, Bipin Chandra Pal and Annie Besant became good friends with senior Leaguers like Jinnah, Mohammad Ali, Raja of Mahmudabad, Raja of Jehangirabad and others. Maulana Mohammad Ali, who was an ardent advocate of Muslim separatism and Bengal's Partition, one who had even questioned the "honesty of the declaration of unity of men, like Mr. Tilak" in 1908, wrote a letter to the same Tilak eight years later in the wake of the Lucknow Pact. "I must confess I had long been a prey to grave misgivings about the catholicity of your political and social ideals and the extent of the connotation of your patriotism. I confess this all the more readily today, because long before today, I learnt to regret these misgivings and have already offered my apologies to you in the spirit, if not in the flesh... Your courage, resolution and fortitude are an example to us younger men...," he wrote.[19]

In their eagerness to win over the League from the British, the Congress leadership missed the point that this bonhomie was a product of their surrender before the separatist demands of the League, and in the process, they converted the Independence movement into a grand bargain with the League. They also missed the point that the correct way to deal with the League was by drawing more Muslims into the Congress, rather than pandering to the whims of a handful of elite Leaguers including Jinnah, who were cleverly sailing in two boats, deploying two tongues suitably. The Congress leadership was in such a trance that a leader of the stature of Lokmanya Tilak, who was critical of M.G. Ranade and Gopal Krishna Gokhale for not standing up to Muslim communalism, was overcome by exuberance and declared the League's coming together at Lucknow as "Luck now at Lucknow". Insisting that he represented the "sense of the Hindu community all over India", Tilak averred that he "would not care if the rights of self-government are granted to the Muhammadan community only."[20]

"The Lucknow Pact was a clear admission that the Congress needed the support of a Muslim party before it could speak on behalf of the entire country. This support, the Congress was ready to buy by accepting a mode of election which was against the better judgement of its leaders and was likely to thwart whatever hopes there were evolving for a common nationality in India," bemoaned the biographer of Gandhi, B.R. Nanda.[21]

The Lucknow Pact did not help create a strong national bond between the communities. It instead helped foment more communalism. When the League annual session was held in Calcutta in 1917, the very same leadership that was present at Lucknow a year ago passed another resolution, demanding this time that the principle of weighted representation should not be limited to the central and provincial legislations alone and should be extended to local bodies, government services and even the universities "in the same proportion of the representation accorded in the legislatures"[22]. The logic given was that the Minto-Morley Reforms had mentioned the phrase "at all levels".

The story of appeasement, bargain and abject surrender before the communal forces by the country's greatest hope for Independence – the Congress – wouldn't stop for the next thirty years until we reach that point of no return – the Partition of India.

* * *

What began as a tactical move to wean away the League from the British soon became a conviction with the Congress, that "without Muslim League coming along, there would be no freedom". For the British – without the League joining hands with the Congress, there won't be a united resistance. Both started patronizing the League. The last three decades of the Independence movement were a saga of this race and competitive bargaining with the Muslim League.

There were many Muslim leaders in the Congress at that time. Even Jinnah was a Congress leader and seen as the ambassador of Hindu-Muslim unity. Sadly, in its competitive bargaining for the League's support, the Congress leadership gave up on those sane and secular Muslim leaders and leaned more and more on the communal and fundamentalist elements in the community.

Reference—

1. *Singh, Jaswant (2009) "Jinnah – India, Partition, Independence" pp. 87, Rupa Publications India Pvt. Ltd.*
2. *Matthews Roderick, "Jinnah Vs. Gandhi" pp. 71, Hachette India.*
3. *Jalal, Ayesha (1994) "The Sole Spokesman: Jinnah, The Muslim League and The Demand for Pakistan" Cambridge University Press*
4. *Pirzada, Syed Sharifuddin (1984), "The Collected Works of Quaid-e-Azam Mohammad Ali Jinnah: Vol-1" p. 2, East and West Publishing Company*
5. *Rana, Vijay (2009), "Jinnah: Facts and Fiction about the Ambassador of Hindu Muslim Unity" available at https://indiabriefings.com/jinnah-facts-and-fiction-about-the-ambassador-of-hindu-muslim-unity/*
6. *Noorani, A.G. (2005), "Jinnah in Indian History" Frontline Magazine, August 12, 2005*
7. *Matthews Roderick, "Jinnah Vs. Gandhi" pp. 16, Hachette India.*
8. *Nanda, B.R. (1989), "Gandhi: Pan-Islamism, Imperialism and NationalismIn India" p. 82, Oxford University Press, Delhi*
9. *Nanda, B.R. (1989), "Gandhi: Pan-Islamism, Imperialism and Nationalism In India" p. 109-110, Oxford University Press, Delhi*
10. *Nanda, B.R. (1989), "Gandhi: Pan-Islamism, Imperialism and Nationalism In India" p. 127, Oxford University Press, Delhi*
11. *Khaliquzzman (1961) "Pathway to Pakistan" pp. 39, Longmans Pakistan Branch*
12. *"Through Indian Eyes" Times of India, April 26, 1924*

13. *Nanda, B.R. (1989), "Gandhi: Pan-Islamism, Imperialism and Nationalism In India" p. 114, Oxford University Press, Delhi*
14. *Ibid.*
15. *Azad, Abulkalam (1940), "Presidential Address: Indian National Congress, 53rd Session, Ramgarh" p. 28-29, Ramgarh Congress; Ed. Zaidi, AM (1985) "Congress Presidential Address: Volume Five: 1940-1985" p. 17-38, Indian Institute of Applied Political Research, New Delhi*
16. *Rana, Vijay (2009), "Jinnah: Facts and Fiction about the Ambassador of Hindu Muslim Unity" available at https://indiabriefings.com/jinnah-facts-and-fiction-about-the-ambassador-of-hindu-muslim-unity/*
17. *"Mohammad Ali Jinnah – An Ambassador of Unity: His Speeches and Writing: 1912-1917" p. 48, Ganesh and Co., Madras,*
18. *"Report of the Indian National Congress: 1906" p. 120*
19. *Nanda, B.R. (1989), "Gandhi: Pan-Islamism, Imperialism and Nationalism In India" p. 142, Oxford University Press, Delhi*
20. *Nanda, B.R. (1989), "Gandhi: Pan-Islamism, Imperialism and Nationalism In India" p. 97, Oxford University Press, Delhi*
21. *Ibid.*
22. *Pirazada, Syed Sharifuddin (1969), "Foundations of Pakistan: All India Muslim League Documents" Vol. 1, National Publishing House*

□

Khilafat Becomes Indian Question

There is among Indians no passion for unity, no desire for fusion. There is no desire to have a common language. There is no will to give up what is local and particular for something which is common and national.

—Dr. B.R. Ambedkar

Into the quagmire walked in another significant leader – Mohandas Gandhi.

Born on October 2, 1869, at Porbandar in Gujarat, to a politician father, Karamchand, who was the Diwan of Porbandar, Mohandas moved to London for studying law and became a lawyer at a young age of twenty-two. After having moved to South Africa in order to represent the case of a wealthy merchant of Indian origin in 1893, Gandhi spent the next twenty-two years there, using not only his professional but political acumen to fight for the rights of the colored peoples of South Africa against the oppressive and unjust regime of the White colonialists.

Thus, by the time he decided to return to India, he had already become a celebrity and was given the acronym of the Mahatma – Great Soul – in 1914, by his followers at Durban. (Indian textbooks attribute it to Rabindranath Tagore, who called Gandhi by that acronym in 1915 in his autobiography in response to Gandhi calling him 'Vishwa Kavi'. The Gujarat High Court too, in a judgment in 1999, confirmed the same[1]). On January 9, 1915, when Gandhi landed at Bombay, he was accorded a grand reception in honour of the fight he had waged in support of the immigrant Indians for the previous two decades.

While in South Africa, Gandhi was following the anti-British movement in India led by the Indian National Congress. He used to occasionally send delegations to the annual Congress sessions held in different Indian cities. Gopal Krishna Gokhale was his political *guru*, who in his address to the twenty-fourth session of the Congress at Lahore, described him in glowing terms as "a man among men, a hero among heroes, a patriot among patriots, and one may well say that in him Indian humanity has reached its high watermark."[2]

Gandhi attended the thirtieth annual Congress session at Bombay in December 1915, where he moved a resolution dealing with the grievances of the Indian immigrants in the British colonies. G.A. Natesan, a well-known editor of the *Indian Review*, published from Madras, used his eloquence to introduce Gandhi and supported the resolution, saying, "The brave and victorious general, Mr. Gandhi has just returned to his motherland after winning a brave feat of arms with weapons unique and almost unparalleled in the history of the world. There happen to be present, on this very platform, two of Mr. Gandhi's distinguished colleagues, Imam Saheb Abdul Kadir Babaji and Sorab Rustomji, the son of that famous passive resister. The problem of Indian nationality, for the solution of which this Congress has been started and for which it has been working with a single-eyed devotion, seems to be very satisfactorily solved in

South Africa with such brave leaders as Mr. Gandhi".[3]

This speech of Natesan is important to understand the perspective of the Congress leadership at the time of Gandhi's entry into Indian political space. It identified Gandhi's struggle against the colonial British in South Africa with that of the Congress' struggle in India. Additional symbolism came from the fact that two of Gandhi's colleagues from South Africa, who sat next to him, were a Muslim and a Parsee. Thus, Gandhi entered the scene with a rather flawed mindset, assuming that the unity of the Indian masses under his leadership was a foregone reality. It also perfectly suited the thinking of the Congress leadership at that time, which was, by then, convinced that no price is big for Hindu-Muslim unity, without which "no freedom is possible".

Gandhi's struggle against racial discrimination in South Africa's Indian enclaves, like Natal and Transvaal, was supported by not only the Hindus, but also by the Muslims and the Parsees. The Transvaal British Indian Association, which stood behind Gandhi in all his struggles, was led by businessmen like Essop Mianand Cachalia; Imam Abdul Bawazeer, a priest; and Dawood Mohamed, a wealthy trader. Gandhi was held in very high esteem by all the Muslims and would occasionally address them in their mosque too – a rare honour for a non-Muslim.

His experience in South Africa convinced Gandhi that he would be able to bring Hindus and Muslims together on one platform in the fight against the colonists. Gandhi chose the twenty-second annual session of the Congress at Surat, in 1907, to drive home this point by sending an all-Muslim delegation from South Africa. In a letter to his mentor,

Gokhale, Gandhi wrote, "May I draw your attention to the fact that the struggle we are undergoing here has resulted in making us feel that we are Indians first, and Hindus, Mahomedans, Tamils, Parsees, etc. You will notice, too, that all our delegates are Mahomedans. I am personally glad of the fact. And it may also happen that there will be many Mahomedans having South African connections, attending the Congress. May I ask you to interest yourself in them and make them feel perfectly at home? A Hindu-Mahomedan compact may even become a special feature of this (Surat) Congress".[4]

It did not become the 'special feature' of Surat Congress, but by the time Gandhi set his foot on the Indian soil, it did. The Lucknow Pact of 1916 was that 'special feature' that Gandhi had envisioned. "My South African experiences had convinced me" Gandhi wrote in his autobiography, "that it would be on the question of Hindu-Muslim unity that my Ahimsa will be put to its severest test"[5].

That Gandhi came to India with this mind can be further illustrated from a meeting held to welcome him to India in Bombay in January 1915. The Gujarati Samaj of Bombay was the host and they invited Jinnah to chair the function. Learning about it Gandhi was 'impressed' that a Muslim was chairing his program. In South Africa, Gujaratis did not include Parsees and Mohammedans, but now he found a Muslim chairing the session that proved that not all Gujaratis were Hindus[6].

Incidentally, as Gandhi entered the Indian National Congress in 1915, some of its senior leaders were removed from the scene by the quirk of fate. Three Congress Moderates died in quick succession. Gokhale died just a month after

Gandhi returned, in February 1915. Pherozeshah Mehta too passed away in November, the same year. Dadabhai Naoroji passed away in 1917. Renowned extremist Congress leader Lokmanya Tilak too left for London to fight his libel suit against Valentine Chirol, the British journalist who called him "the father of India's unrest". Tilak spent full ten months in London and died in 1920, after his return.

Thus, the leadership of the Congress, with the Lucknow Pact mindset dominating the thinking of the Moderates, effortlessly fell in the lap of Gandhi. To his credit, Gandhi was recognised neither as a Moderate nor as an Extremist. He was not recognised as a major force in the first couple of years of his entry. Infact, the visiting Secretary of State Montagu commented in 1917 that Gandhi was just a "social reformer with a real desire to find grievances and to cure them not for any reasons of self-advertisement, but to improve the conditions of his fellow-countrymen. He dresses like a coolie, forswears all personal advancement, lives practically on the air and is a pure visionary".[7] Looking at Gandhi's fads and peculiarities, Viceroy Chelmsford even told him in 1918, "There will be none to agree with you or follow you."

Chelmsford was right. Gandhi came in with a sense of superiority overawed by his successes in South Africa and his techniques like Ahimsa and Satyagraha – non-violence and truthful resistance. His first meeting with Jinnah in India at the Gujarati reception ended on a sour note when Gandhi interrupted the latter when he rose to speak in English and insisted on Gujarati. Jinnah ignored the suggestion, but a seed of discord was sown. Stanley Wolpert, author of one of the best biographies on Jinnah, was tempted to read the future gulf between the two leaders in this very first encounter. It led to both see each other as "natural enemies"[8], he wrote.

A year later, in February 1916, Malviya invited Gandhi to the opening ceremony of the Benaras Hindu University in Kashi. This institution was originally started by Anne Besant in 1892, but had since been upgraded to a university status. Viceroy Hardinge was present, so were many Congress luminaries including Anne Besant, rich donars, representatives of the royals and other aristocracy who were supporting Malviya in building the institution. Gandhi's speech was a frontal attack, at times personal criticism at almost everyone in the audience.

"He berated the rajas and aristocrats for their ostentatious jewellery; he regretted that the educated elite chose to learn and conduct their politics in English; he criticized the heavy security that surrounded the Viceroy, asking whether this was any way to build trust, or for the Viceroy, trapped in such a 'living death', to not have any kind of contact with the Indian people in his charge; he bemoaned the dirty state of India's temples and asked what good it would do such places if the British left tomorrow – would they somehow suddenly become clean and wholesome? In response to this verbal attack, there were howls of dissent from the floor and the podium, but cheers from some of the students. Offended dignitaries walked out and Anne Besant begged him to stop", wrote Roderick[9].

Some cheered Gandhi for his frankness and uprightness. Some felt Gandhi was mad. That was the reaction of the British Prime Minister Sir John Lloyd when he received a message from Gandhi requesting him to sign on the Swadeshi pledge. "I have received a note from Gandhi asking me if I will sign the Swadeshi pledge which he is just about to issue and assuring me that my sympathy and signature will be of immense value. I really think the Mahatma is rapidly going mad", he wrote to Secretary Edwin Montagu in May 1919. Some felt that Gandhi was overconfident about his ability based on his South Africa experience and also in a hurry. But very few realized that there was a method in his seeming madness. Lloyd again writes to Montagu three weeks later, correcting himself this time and saying that "I am afraid he (Gandhi) is really pretty wicked, as cunning as a fox and at heart bitterly anti-British"[10].

Anne Besant and other had launched Home Rule Movement in 1916 at Calcutta on the lines of the Irish Home Rule League to promote political education about self-rule among the masses of India. Jinnah was also a part of the group. He recommended Gandhi's name for its presidency. Some leaders like M.R. Jayakar were opposed to Gandhi for his "pet theories" and "fantastic fads", but Gandhi managed to overcome the opposition and became the president in 1919. But as soon as he became the president, Gandhi set aside the objections of all the other seniors and changed the name of the organization to "Swarajya Sabha". He also proposed to amend its constitution by changing the central demand from that of home rule to complete self-government. Those were not necessarily bad moves, but hasty no doubt.

Irritated by Gandhi's unilateralism, both Jinnah and Besant resigned. When Gandhi asked Jinnah to reconsider, Jinnah declined saying that he could not accept Gandhi's methods and programs, which would surely "lead to disaster and chaos"[11]. Ironically, a year later, circumstances propelled Gandhi to the centerstage of the Indian freedomstruggle .

* * *

Gandhi's entry into Indian political theatre was treated as a small affair by senior Congress leaders of the time, but he received enthusiastic support from the Muslim community in several places. When he visited the Aligarh Muslim University in November 1917, he received an enthusiastic reception from students, who released the horses of his carriage and pulled it through the decorated streets by themselves. Gandhi also made it a point to attend the Muslim League sessions which were being held at the same place as the Congress sessions. He was there at the Calcutta League session in December 1917, supporting the Lucknow Pact and also throwing his weight behind the Ali Brothers who were incarcerated by the British at Chindwara in Central Provinces.

The First World War was ending, and the treatment meted out to Turkey and its Ottoman Sultan Mehmed V was agitating the Muslims in India. Gandhi noticed how intimately Ali Brothers and other Leaguers were associated with the cause of the Ottoman Sultan, whom they considered the Khalifa of the Muslim world. Mohammad Ali wrote a letter to Viceroy Lord Chelmsford stating that the Turkish situation had left the Indian Muslims with only two options – *jihad* (holy war) or *hijrat* (leaving India). Ali Brothers were still in jail and Gandhi was one of the persistent demanders of their release to the chagrin of the British, who wouldn't see any logic in him meddling in the pan-Islamist business of the Ali Brothers.

Gandhi was preparing to launch his first-ever Indian version of the non-violent *satyagraha* against the Rowlatt Act, promulgated by the British in early 1919, which gave powers to the British regime to arrest anyone under the charge of terrorism and keep in jail for two years without trial. Non-violence of Gandhi was new to the Indian masses. Two months into *satyagraha*, there was violence in several places, like Bombay, Ahmedabad and Amritsar. Gandhi immediately suspended the agitation.

On their part, Muslim League leaders, like Maulana Abdul Bari took the lead in mobilizing the support of Indian Muslims for the cause of the restoration of the Khalifa of Turkey. A Khilafat committee was formed in March 1919, and October 17, 1919 was declared as the All-India Khilafat Day. Abdul Bari was a hardliner and a fundamentalist Muslim leader, who had declared open *jhad* against the Hindus in the wake of the communal riots in Bihar, in 1917. When he saw Gandhi in a loin cloth for the first time, Bari burst out saying "It is against our scriptures to keep the knees bare in this fashion"[12]. Later, he befriended Gandhi and sought his support for the Khilafat cause. Khilafat Day was a great success, with Hindus also participating in it in large numbers.

Thus was born a new pan-Islamist movement on Indian soil with the tacit support of Gandhi and the Congress leadership. This turned the Indian Muslim opinion forever into a pan-Islamist one.

Khilafat was a religio-political movement launched by a section of the League Muslims for the preservation of the Ottoman Empire under Sultan Mehmed V and the restoration of the Khalifa (leader) of the entire Muslim *ummah* (religious community). Sir Jadunath Sarkar, eminent historian of those times, clearly stated that "the theory that the Muslim ruler of Turkey is the spiritual head of all

Muhammadens, is a creation of the late nineteenth century, and merely a result of the growth of a political pan-Islamic movement as a natural reaction against steady absorption of all sovereign Muslim states by the Christians."[13]

It should be clear from the description that, one, it was a religious movement; and two, it had nothing to do with India's Independence. More importantly, the myth of the Ottoman emperor as the Khalifa of the world's Muslims had been shattered by the dismantling of the empire by the British after the First World War and subsequently when Mustafa Kemal Pasha, the newly elected leader of Turkey, abolished the title of Khalifa in 1924.

That was what Jinnah told the Muslim League convention held in Delhi, in 1918. Jinnah called Khilafat as a "false religious frenzy of which no good will come out for India."[14] When some members objected to his views, and the League decided to form a Khilafat Committee to launch an agitation for the cause, Jinnah, along with some others, walked out of the session.

Not just Jinnah, but several other Muslim groups too rejected the call for restoration of the Khalifa. Maulana Ahmed Raza Khan Barelvi, renowned Islamic scholar and philosopher, had issued a fatwa opining that since the Ottomans were not from Prophet Muhammad's Quraish tribe, they could not claim to be caliphs of Islam. The Ahmadiyya community welcomed the defeat of the Ottoman Sultan by holding celebrations in their holy city of Qadian in Punjab[15].

In his famous book, Thy Hand, Great Anarch, renowned author Nirad C. Chaudhuri describes Khilafat volunteers as "recruited from the lowest Muslim riffraff... brandishing their whips at people"[16].

But where Jinnah walked out, Gandhi walked in one year later. The All India Khilafat Committee, headquartered in Lucknow, felt that it needed the support of the Hindus to build a strong campaign. Gandhi immediately came forward and he was elected as the president of the Khilafat Committee. For him, it was an opportunity to bring Muslims into the freedom movement.

Several Congress leaders participated in the Khilafat Day protests organised by the Muslim League on 17 October, 1919. Swami Shraddhananda, a renowned Arya Samaj leader and a senior Congress leader was one among them, standing on the steps of the Jama Masjid in Delhi and exhorting the Muslims to fight for the Khilafat. Gandhi, along with Motilal Nehru, Madan Mohan Malviya and others, was present at the Muslim League convention in December 1919. He described Khilafat as the 'holy cow' of the Muslim community. He viewed Khilafat as the best opportunity for Hindu-Muslim unity and exhorted the Hindus to join the struggle for preserving Islam's honour if they really wanted Muslims' friendship. "Arise! Awake! Or be fallen forever," was Gandhi's call to the Muslims.

However, a section of the Congressmen started raising concerns over this gamble. Sardar Patel was unconvinced about a slave country fighting for the freedom of the Arabs elsewhere. "Imagine our fighting for the independence of the Arabs in Arabia and Palestine, Syria and Mesopotamia, when we ourselves are held as slaves under the British bayonets," Patel said wryly.[17] Gandhi's good friend Barrister Henry Pollack warned that on the Khilafat question, Gandhi was behaving in an "ill-informed and dangerous manner".

"Some Hindu leaders like Madan Mohan Malviya

recoiled from the very idea of involving Hindus in a purely religious crusade of the Muslim community. They had been shaken by the assertion of Hasrat Mohani and Shaukat Ali that it was legitimate for Indian Muslims to support an Afghan invasion of India in the interest of the Khilafat. To Rabindranath Tagore, the agitation was a manifestation of irrational and turbulent politics," wrote B.R. Nanda.[18]

But Gandhi was unrelenting. "The Khilafat has become an Indian question. It is no longer merely a Muslim grievance", he wrote in September 1920[19].

"If twenty-two crores of Hindus intelligently plead for the Muslims on the Khilafat issue, I believe they would forever win the vote of eight crores of Muslims," he argued. It was an open bargain now.[20]

* * *

A couple of days later, U.P. Provincial Khilafat Conference was organised at Meerut in March 1920. Gandhi was present in the conference. It was here that Gandhi announced non-cooperation as one of the programmes against the government. It is important to note that although influential, Gandhi did not hold any formal post in Congress at that time. He built a friendship with the Khilafatist leadership, committed the support of Congress and later made it a *fait accompli* for the Congress to pass a resolution in its favour in August and December 1920.

An emergency session of the Congress was called a few months later, in August 1920, at Calcutta, where Gandhi proposed to launch a nationwide non-cooperation movement in support of the Khilafat. "I would, in order to achieve success in the Khilafat issue, even postpone the issue of *swaraj*," he declared. Leaders like Chittaranjan

Das, Bipin Chandra Pal and Anne Besant were against this bargain. When the Provincial Congress Committees were asked to give their opinion, only one, the Sindh PCC, supported Gandhi's programme. Finally, it was the support of the Muslim delegates that saw the Khilafat resolution through. To assuage the sentiments of naysayers, issues like *swaraj* and Jallianwala Bagh massacre were also included to make it look like an agitation for the Indian cause.

Gandhi hoped that the Indian Muslims would, like the Muslims in South Africa, religiously follow his programme of non-violent non-cooperation. However, the hotheads in the Khilafat committees, like Maulana Abdul Bari and Hasrat Mohani, were in no mood to pursue the Gandhian programme. Bari threatened Gandhi that if he failed to deliver on the promise of the Congress' support, they would end their relations with it. "Tell Mr. Gandhi that...we shall not sit (idle) relying upon him, but thanking him for his sympathy, will fulfil our religious obligations," Abdul Bari wrote to Shaukat Ali.[21]

Many others in Congress were also uncomfortable with the Khilafat business of the Muslim League and Gandhi's support to it. The Leader, published from Allahabad, wrote in an editorial that: "The Khilafat has changed hands so many times in Muslim history, without Islam being destroyed. When the Young Turks deposed the late Sultan of Turkey, Abdul Hamid, did they consult the Indian Muslims? Was there any protest in the country against their sacrilegious proceedings? Let Indian Muhammedans be not carried away by catch phrases. Their religion is in no danger. No one is going to interfere with their spiritual allegiance to Khalif. But the doctrine that with the spiritual goes the temporal allegiance is against all commonsense"[22].

Jinnah, who was until then midwifing the Congress-League friendship, got disillusioned. He was particularly upset with his own sidelining in the Muslim League and promotion of Mohammad Ali and Shaukat Ali – the Ali Brothers – by Gandhi. At the Nagpur session of the Congress later that year, egged on by Motilal and others, he stood up to challenge Gandhi. But it was not easy. Most of the senior Congress leaders, including Motilal Nehru, Madan Mohan Malviya and Lala Lajpat Rai developed cold feet and simply sided with Gandhi in the last minute. Roderick Matthews writes that "Kanji Dwarkadas, an eyewitness, recounts how Jinnah was asked directly by Motilal and others to speak out against Gandhi on behalf of them all. Jinnah obliged, but Motilal and his supporters deserted him and voted with the platform on the day. This act of betrayal certainly isolated Jinnah among the Congress leadership and may have been a factor in his decision not only to leave but also not to rejoin"[23].

The new friends of Gandhi among the Muslim Leaguers, like the Ali Brothers, whose friendship with Gandhi was resented strongly by Jinnah, rose to Gandhi's defence.

When Jinnah tried to speak up against the Khilafat, he was challenged and humiliated. He insisted on addressing Gandhi as 'Mr. Gandhi', while those on the dais insisted that he should address him as 'Mahatma Gandhi'. Occasionally, Jinnah did use the word 'Mahatma', but what angered the League leaders on the dias was his refusal to address Mohammad Ali as 'Maulana'. When Jinnah refused to call his brother a Maulana, Shaukat Ali rushed towards him with the intention of an assault. Maulana Mohammad Ali ridiculed him over his insistence on constitutional means. "The Maulana narrated a story linking Jinnah with a preacher of the Salvation Army, who went on declaring 'Come this way – the God's way'. Someone asked him: 'How long have you been saying this?'. He replied, 'twenty years.' The man retorted: 'If after twenty years, it has got you where you are, I don't think much of it'. Finding the atmosphere hostile, Jinnah walked out of the meeting, never to return to Congress," writes Rafiq Zakaria.[24]

Jinnah resigned, using his opposition to the Khilafat as an excuse. "I will have nothing to do with this pseudo-religious approach to politics. I do not believe in working up mob hysteria; politics is a gentleman's game," Jinnah said, while quitting.[25]

"Your methods have already caused split and division in almost every institution that you have approached hitherto, and in the public life of the country not only amongst Hindus and Muslims But between Hindus and Hindus and Muslims and Muslims and even between fathers and sons; people generally are desperate all over the country and your extreme programme has for the moment struck the imagination mostly of the inexperienced youth and the ignorant and the illiterate", wrote Jinnah to Gandhi, pouring out his grudge against the new entrant[26].

Years later, Gandhi recalls Jinnah telling him that he had "ruined politics in India by dragging up a lot of unwholesome elements in Indian life and giving them political prominence, that it was a crime to mix up politics and religion the way he had done"[27].

Gandhi's dominant role in the Nagpur session was noticed by the British officials also. Sir Frank Sly, who was the Chief Commissioner of the Central Provinces, wrote to Viceroy that, "The outstanding feature of the Congress has been the personal domination of Gandhi over all political leaders and followers alike. All opposition to his views has been overcome without difficulty, owing to his strong hold over the bulk of the delegates.... The moderates of Nagpur were not heard; the extremist opponents under Kharpade and Dr. Munje were brushed aside; Pandit Madan Mohan Malviya's effort was nugatory; Jinnah carried no influence; Lajpat Roy wobbled, and then became silent. I understand their view to be that it was hopeless to attempt any real opposition in the temper of the meeting"[28].

Khilafat failed. But the non-cooperation movement that Gandhi launched, although hastily withdrawn, changed the character of the independence movement. Days of well-dressed elites writing endless memorandums to the British mandarins through constitutional means were replaced by aggressive mass politics that defied all constitutional rules and regulations. Gandhi had not only transformed how Congress works, even how it looks. The Congressmen started wearing Khadi or simple attire henceforth. That was the greatest contribution of Gandhi to the remainder of India's freedom struggle.

The non-cooperation movement was abruptly called off by Gandhi when a violent incident took place at Chauri Chaura in the Gorakhpur district of United Provinces in which twenty-two policemen were killed by the agitators. However, the damage to the fabric of national unity was already done. After the Khilafat, voices of the nationalist Muslims became further subdued. Muslim communalism not only became the order of the day but was even condoned by the Congress leadership.

Khilafat was the only religious cause that Gandhi ever

espoused during the Independence movement. He probably had his reasons for doing so.

"The passions he had helped rouse, which were now turned against him and the Congress, meant that the Congress hemorrhaged Muslims ever afterwards. Gandhi returned to the secular straight-and-narrow with the salt *satyagraha* ten years later and strove manfully to secure the Moderate's aim of a pluralist nationalism in the age of mass politics, but opportunism of the Khilafat movement haunted the Congress and helped alienate the one constituency it prized above all others: India's Muslims," wrote Mukul Keshavan[29].

The Khilafat misadventure of the Congress had demonstrated that the seeds of communal separatism sown by the British a decade earlier were sprouting up, actively nurtured by the misplaced convictions of the Congress leadership. Later events led to further communalization of Muslim politics as the Congress continued its appeasement policies.

* * *

While the long-time fallout of the ill-advised Khilafat was experienced by the nation in 1940s, the immediate fallout was witnessed in one remote southern corner, in the Malabar region of Kerala. The Moplah or Mapilla Rebellion, as described in the history of India's Independence movement, was one of the bloodiest fallouts of the Khilafat.

Distortion of history is a trade in which the fascists and the communists excel. They presented the Moplah Rebellion as a rebellion against the British, while pushing the gory communal orgy of the Muslims of Malabar under the carpet.

Fascists are known for blatant distortion of history; the Communists are one step ahead. They not only distort history with impunity but blame their opponents as fascists. Stalin blamed Jews as fascists. Brezhnev called the entire capitalist West as fascist. In India, the nationalists are fascists for them. Talking of distorting history, Stalin demanded that 1941 should be projected as the year of Soviet Union's entry into the Second World War. His intimacy with the Nazi buddy Hitler during 1939-41, invasion of Poland in 1939 and Baltic States in 1940, massacre of thousands of Poles at Katyn in 1940, were all pushed under the carpet.

Russian President Putin promulgated a law that criminalised talking about the incidents of 1939-41. The Russian Supreme Court went one step further and made even a re-posting of such material a punishable crime. Historian Timothy Snyder called this behaviour as 'schizofascism'.[30] The latest case of schizofascism in india was the attempt to whitewash the history of Moplah atrocities of 1921.

Moplahs, descendants of the early Muslim migrants from Arabia, lived in large numbers in the Malabar region of north Kerala. In 1921, they were estimated to number around 300,000 and constituted a third of the Malabar population. Moplah leaders were fanatical and violent. Even the senior Left leader EMS Namboodiripad had referred to this streak in his book, *Keralathinde Desheeya Prashnam* (Kerala's National Problem). There were religious fanatics "who believed killing or converting a *kafir* will take them to the steps leading to the threshold of heaven," he wrote.[31]

The Congress leaders in Kerala, like K. Madhavan Nair and U. Gopala Menon took the lead in taking the non-cooperation and Khilafat movements to different parts of Kerala. A Malabar Khilafat Committee was formed in January 1921 under the leadership of Mahadum Tangal, the highest religious authority of the Moplahs. Moplah leaders plunged into the Khilafat movement. Soon Khilafat committees were formed in a number of Muslim villages across Malabar. Moplahs were not particularly known for non-violence. Six months after the committees were formed, tensions rose in the region. Ali Musliar, a religious preacher from village Tirurangadi, led thousands of Khilafat volunteers in processions that threatened peace and pushed minority Hindus into fear. The *Madras Mail* reported that a large proportion of the demonstrators were "armed with war knives, spears, country swords and other weapons including some guns."

Sensing that the violent activities of the Moplah leaders in the name of Khilafat were forcing Hindus to withdraw, Gandhi decided to undertake a visit to the region along with Shaukat Ali, leader of the Khilafat movement. While Gandhi advocated peaceful resistance, Shaukat Ali resorted to the language of *jihad*. Kunjahmad Hazi, the prominent face of the Moplahs, refused to join the Congress movement, blaming its 'Hindu credentials.' Instead, he launched the Khilafat movement in August 1921. Knives, swords and other deadly weapons were manufactured in large numbers. Large-scale violence and arson were unleashed. Hazi, together with Ali Musaliar, declared the establishment of Islamic Khilafat (Caliphate) in two *tehsils* – Ernad and Valluvanad.

While in Turkey, the Ottoman Khalifa was deposed by secular leaders, like Mustafa Kemal Pasha, the In Malabar, Khilafat was revived and offered to the Congress leadership, not *swarajya*.

The British came down heavily on the Moplahs. According to official estimates, 2,339 Moplahs were killed and 1,652 wounded. Moplahs turned their anger against minority Hindus. They were blamed as collaborators with the British. The ensuing four months became a living hell for the Hindus of Malabar. "Imbichi Koya Thangal, who was also operating in Walluvanad *taluk*, awarded capital punishment to thirty eight Hindus, whose only crime was that they had supplied milk and coconuts to the army," wrote K.M. Panikkar, quoting a Malayali book of K. Madhavan Nair, *Malabar Kalapam*.

Hundreds of Hindus were killed, and thousands forcefully converted to Islam. Contemporary British records and media coverage provide vivid description of the atrocities. Media wrote about dozens of camps set up for over one lakh displaced. Malayalam writers reflected Moplah horrors in their writings. In a poem written in 1922, Kumaranashan, a close disciple of Sree Narayana Guru, explicitly blamed the Moplahs for atrocities. "*Kollakkarottale vettikolacheythum Allah mathathil pidichu cherthum*", means "the looters hacked many to death and forcibly converted others to the religion of Allah", he wrote.

The women of Malabar shot off a desperate letter to the wife of Viceroy Reading. "Your Ladyship is not fully apprised of all the horrors and atrocities perpetrated by the fiendish rebels: of the many wells and tanks filled up with the mutilated but often only half-dead bodies of our nearest and dearest ones who refused to abandon the faith of our fathers; of pregnant women cut to pieces and left on the roadside and in the jungles, with the unborn babe protruding from the mangled corpse; of our innocent and helpless children torn from our arms and done to death before our eyes and our husbands and fathers tortured, flayed and burnt alive; of thousands of our homesteads reduced to cinder mounds; of our places of worship desecrated and destroyed and of the images of the deity shamefully insulted by putting the entrails of slaughtered cows, or else smashed to pieces; of the wholesale looting of hard-earned wealth of generations, reducing many who were formerly rich and prosperous to publicly beg in the streets of Calicut," they wrote.[32]

In a letter to Gandhi on September 8, 1921, senior Congress leader of Madras, C. Rajagopalachari, wrote: "The doings of Moplah bands have made man, woman and child among the Hindus lose faith in Hindu-Muslim unity."[33]

Ambedkar was more forthright. "The Hindus were visited by a dire fate at the hands of the Moplahs. Massacres, forcible conversions, desecration of temples, foul outrages upon women, such as ripping open pregnant women, pillage, arson and destruction – in short, all the accompaniments of brutal and unrestrained barbarism, were perpetrated freely by the Moplahs upon the Hindus," he wrote.[34]

However, Kunjahmad Hazi, in a letter to *The Hindu* in October 1921, flatly denied any wrongdoing. He resorted to victim-shaming, accusing Hindus of conniving with the British and handing over the hiding Moplahs to them, for which only "a few Hindus have been put to some trouble".[35] Hasrat Mohani, who was presiding over the Muslim League session in Ahmedabad at that time, defended the Moplah atrocities against the Hindus as acts of 'self-defence'.

But Congress' reaction was strange. The Madras Provincial Congress constituted a committee to look into the Moplah atrocities and it concluded that the district officials of south Malabar were at fault. When the AICC met at Ahmedabad in December 1921, the entire effort seemed to downplay the atrocities by the Moplahs. While the Servants of India Society, led by Anne Besant, reported that over 20,000 Hindus were forcefully converted to Islam, the Congress claimed that as per their information, only three people were converted. The Ahmedabad session of the Congress witnessed a lot of tussles between the Congress and League members over the Moplah incidents. All that could be said in the resolution was that the Congress "...is of the opinion that the...disturbance in Malabar could have been prevented by the government of Madras accepting the proffered assistance of Maulana Yakub Hassan." "The outbreak would not have occurred had the message of non-violence been allowed to reach them," it argued.[36]

Describing the events at the session, Swami Shraddhanand, who was enthusiastically championing the Khilafat cause until then, wrote, "The original resolution condemned the Moplas wholesale for the killing of Hindus and burning of Hindu homes and the forcible conversion to Islam. The Hindu members themselves proposed amendments till it was reduced to condemning only certain individuals who had been guilty of the above crimes. But some of the Moslem leaders could not bear this even. Maulana Fakir and other Maulanas, of course, opposed the resolution and there was no wonder. But I was surprised, an out-and-out nationalist like Maulana Hasrat Mohani opposed the resolution on the ground that the Mopla country no longer remained Dar-ul-Aman but became Dar-ul-Harab and they suspected the Hindus of collusion with the British enemies of the Moplahs. Therefore, the Moplas were right in presenting the Quran or sword to the Hindus. And if the Hindus became Mussalmans to save themselves from death, it was a voluntary change of faith and not forcible conversion – well, even the harmless resolution condemning some of the Moplas was not unanimously passed but had to be accepted by a majority of votes only."[37]

All this was done for the sake of keeping the League as a bedfellow. The final hit on the nail was the reaction of Gandhi, who, incidentally, became the sole executive authority in the Congress from this session onwards.

"What happened in Malabar is gnawing our minds. My heart bleeds when I think whether our Muslim brethren have gone mad," a shocked Gandhi bemoaned.[38] But he was not ready to denounce the Moplahs, whom he described as 'brave'. In his opinion, they simply "mistook the mission of the Khilafat".

"The Moplahs were never particularly friendly to the Malabar Hindus. They had looted them before. They were kept in utter darkness by the government and neglected by both Mussalmans and Hindus. Being wild and brave but ignorant, they have mistaken the mission of Khilafat and acted in a savage, inhuman and irreligious manner," Gandhi concluded.[39]

"Be the Moplahs be ever so bad, they deserve to be treated as humans," Gandhi appealed.[40]

In Dr. Ambedkar's words, "Mr. Gandhi was so much obsessed by the necessity of establishing Hindu-Muslim unity that he was prepared to make light of the doings of the Moplas and the Khilafats who were congratulating them. He spoke of the Mappilas as the 'brave God-fearing Moplahs who were fighting for what they consider as religion and in a manner which they consider as religious'."[41]

Reference—

1. *"Gujarat High Court Clarifies "Rabindranath Tagore Gave Mahatama Title To Gandhi"For Query Of Rajkot Job Exam" accessed at https://www.gujaratheadline.com/gujarat-high-court-clarifies-rabindranath%E2%80%8B-tagore-gave-mahatma-title-to-gandhi-for-query-of-rajkot-talati-exam/*
2. *Nanda, B.R. (1989), "Gandhi: Pan-Islamism, Imperialism and Nationalism In India" p. 146, Oxford University Press, Delhi*
3. *"Report of the Thirteenth Indian National Congress" 1915, p. 65-66, Jt. Hon. Secy. Bombay Presidency Association*
4. *Nanda, B.R. (1989), "Gandhi: Pan-Islamism, Imperialism and Nationalism In India" p. 4, Oxford University Press, Delhi*
5. *Gandhi, M K (1925) "The Story of my Experiments with Truth" pp. 539-540*
6. *Gandhi, M.K. "The Collected Works of Mahatama Gandhi" Vol. 14, pp. 342-343, Gandhi Sevagram Ashram.*
7. *Nanda, B.R. (1989), "Gandhi: Pan-Islamism, Imperialism and Nationalism In India" p. 165, Oxford University Press, Delhi*
8. *Wolpert, Stanley (1984)"Jinnah of Pakistan" pp. 38, Oxford University Press*
9. *Matthews, Roderick "Jinnah vs Gandhi" pp. 81, Hachette India*
10. *Nanda, B.R. (1989), "Gandhi: Pan-Islamism, Imperialism and Nationalism In India" pp. 194, Oxford University Press, Delhi*
11. *Wolpert, Stanley (1984) "Jinnah of Pakistan" pp. 70, Oxford University Press*
12. *Lelyveld, Joseph (2012), "Great Soul: Mahatama Gandhi and His Struggles with India" pp. 164, Vintage Books*
13. *Nanda, B.R. (1989), "Gandhi: Pan-Islamism, Imperialism and Nationalism In India" p. 211, Oxford University Press, Delhi*
14. *Niemeijer, A.C. (1972), "The Khilafat Movement in India: 1919-1924" p. 90, The Hague – Martin Nijhoff*
15. *Ahmed, Ishtiaq (2020), "Jinnah: His Successed, Failures and Role in History" pp. 65, Penguin*
16. *Chaudhuri, Nirad C (1987), "Thy Hand, Great Anarch! India: 1921-1952" pp. 19, Chatto and Windus, London*
17. *Yajinik, Indulal K (1943) "Gandhi: As I Knew Him" p. 131, S.A. Haider Manager Danish Mahal, Delhi*
18. *Nanda, B.R. (1989), "Gandhi: Pan-Islamism, Imperialism and Nationalism In India" p. 222, Oxford University Press, Delhi*
19. *Gandhi, M.K. "The Collected Works of Mahatama Gandhi" Vol. 21, pp. 63, Gandhi Sevagram Ashram*

20. *Misra, Amalendu (2004), "Identity and Religion: Foundations of Anti-Islamism in India" SAGE Publications*
21. *Nanda, B.R. (1989), "Gandhi: Pan-Islamism, Imperialism and Nationalism In India" p. 219, Oxford University Press, Delhi*
22. *Nanda, B.R. (1989), "Gandhi: Pan-Islamism, Imperialism and Nationalism In India" pp. 221-222, Oxford University Press, Delhi*
23. *Matthews, Roderick "Jinnah vs Gandhi" pp. 249, Hachette India*
24. *Zakaria, Rafiq (1999), "Gandhi and the Break-Up of India" p. 52, Bharatiya Vidya Bhavan*
25. *Tunzelmann, Alex Von (2008), "Indian Summer: The Secret History of the End of an Empire" p. 91, Pocket Books*
26. *Saiyid, M.H. (1962), "Mohammad Ali Jinnah: A Political Study" pp. 264, University of Michigan Press*
27. *Singh, Jaswant (2009), "Jinnah: India-Partition-Independence" pp. 125, Rupa Publications*
28. *Nanda, B.R. (1989), "Gandhi: Pan-Islamism, Imperialism and Nationalism In India" pp. 239-240, Oxford University Press, Delhi*
29. *Madhav, Ram (2020), "Partitioned Freedom: Pari IV" accessed at https://chintan.indiafoundation.in/articles/partitioned-freedom-khilafat-movement/*
30. *Snyder, Timothy (2018), "The Road to Unfreedom: Russia, Europe, America" p. 175, Tim Duggan Books, USA*
31. *Nandakumar, J. (2020), "Moplah riots were a pogrom against Hindus" accessed at https://www.sundayguardianlive.com/opinion/moplah-riots-pogrom-hindus*
32. *Nair, Diwan Bahadur C. Gopalan (1923), "The Moplah Rebellion 1921" pp. 74*
33. *Nanda, B.R. (1989), "Gandhi: Pan-Islamism, Imperialism and Nationalism In India" p. 319, Oxford University Press, Delhi*
34. *Nandakumar, J. (2020), "Moplah riots were a pogrom against Hindus" accessed at https://www.sundayguardianlive.com/opinion/moplah-riots-pogrom-hindus*
35. *"The Letter written by V.K. Haji which appeared in The Hindu on October 18, 1921" accessed at https://www.thehindu.com/news/national/kerala/reports-of-hindu-muslim-strife-in-malabar-baseless/article31918716.ece*
36. *"Report of the Thirty Sixth Indian National Congress" p. 48, Navjeevan Press, Ahmedabad*
37. *Ambedkar, Babasaheb (2021) "Thoughts on Pakistan" p. 155-156, Prabhat Prakashan*
38. *Nandakumar, J. (2020), "Moplah riots were a pogrom against*

Hindus" accessed at https://www.sundayguardianlive.com/opinion/moplah-riots-pogrom-hindus

39. *Nanda, B.R. (1989), "Gandhi: Pan-Islamism, Imperialism and Nationalism In India" p. 320, Oxford University Press, Delhi*
40. *Ibid.*
41. *Ambedkar, Babasaheb (2021) "Thoughts on Pakistan" p. 153, Prabhat Prakashan*

□

Unity As Obsession Appeasement As Mission

A wholly communal organization like the Muslim League has attained parity with a nationalist organization like the Indian National Congress Party.

—Madan Mohan Malviya

Khilafat, non-cooperation, Hindu-Muslim unity – all came to an end with one decision of Gandhi in 1922.

On February 5, 1922, at a place called Chauri Chaura near Gorakhpur in Uttar Pradesh, some two thousand protesters were participating in a non-cooperation event when the police fired upon them. Three civilian protesters were killed in the firing. What happened subsequently was the macabre dance of death. Enraged protesters attacked the local police station and lynched the entire staff inside, including the *chawkidar*. When eight armed policemen were sent to protect the police station, they too were massacred. While a total of seventeen police personnel were killed, five protesters also died, taking the toll of total dead to twenty-two.

Gandhi was shaken. His dream of peaceful resistance had simply crumbled in front of his own eyes. When a few months before, the Moplahs in Malabar indulged in violence, Gandhi was in a mood to allow it to pass. But not this time.

He, who called the rebellious and murderous Moplahs as 'humans', categorized the conduct of the protesters at Chauri Chaura as 'inhuman'. An urgent meeting of the Congress Working Committee was called at Bardoli in Gujarat on February 11, 1922. Gandhi was present, but only a couple of others, like Jamnalal Bajaj and Vithalbhai Patel could make it. A resolution was hurriedly passed, deploring the "inhuman conduct of the mob at Chauri Chaura in having brutally murdered constables and wantonly burnt police *thana*."[1] And then came the shocking decision of suspending the civil disobedience movement.

Just a few days before, Gandhi had given a final ultimatum to the British Government over *swaraj* and Khilafat. The British too were preparing for an intensified agitation in the country. Many Congress and League leaders were already arrested. There were pressures on the Viceroy for the arrest of Gandhi also, but the government was hesitant, fearing widespread reaction if Gandhi were arrested. All this changed suddenly with the decision at Bardoli.

Leaders of the Congress, both Gandhi's admirers and adversaries, were shocked. Rajagopalachari, who was in jail, wrote in his dairy that he failed "to see the logicality of the grave step taken".[2] Motilal Nehru was furious and decided to part ways with Gandhi. Together with Chittaranjan Das, he decided to start a new party, called the Swarajya Party. Even Jawaharlal Nehru, who was in prison for the first time, was very annoyed and shot off an angry letter to Gandhi, which Gandhi later described as a 'freezing dose'.

But the strongest resentment came from the Khilafatists. They felt let down and betrayed. Radical Islamist leaders, like Abdul Bari and Hasrat Mohani, were angry at Gandhi and threw inuendoes at him. Slowly, but steadily, the charade of Congress-League unity was coming to an end. "Hindu-Muslim unity is dying, if not dead," wrote Governor of UP, Harcourt Butler.[3]

But the League leaders didn't give up on their Khilafat dreams. Although the Ottoman Sultan was deposed and Mustafa Kemal Pasha, a secular-minded army general became the new leader of Turkey, the Indian Muslim leaders decided to pursue their goal of reestablishing Khilafat. The Central Khilafat Committee approached Kemal Pasha through a letter in November 1923 with the proposal that he should take over the mantle of new Khalifa.

Kemal Pasha was rather amused and ridiculed them, saying, "They were Muslim peoples, who fought against the Turks under the British flag at the Dardanelles, in Syria and in Iraq".[4] Dismissing their missive, Kemal Pasha retorted, "I gather from your letter that you have been influenced by pernicious propaganda."[5] A few months later, he formally announced the abolition of the office of Khalifa itself, which many attribute to the overenthusiasm of the Indian Khilafat Committee.

Gandhi was finally arrested and sentenced to five years of imprisonment. "Not a dog barked," commented the Viceroy derisively at the lack of protests over his arrest.[6] He was sent to the Yerawada Jail in Pune, where the Khilafatists like Ali Brothers too were incarcerated. While the Khilafatists continued to dream about Khalifa, Gandhi too didn't give up on his dream of Hindu-Muslim unity for the sake of *swaraj*. In jail, in the company of the Khilafat colleagues, Gandhi would religiously observe Muslim festivals like the Eid in the hope that the unconditional support of the Hindus would secure the lasting gratitude and support of the Muslims for the cause of freedom.

But as the later events would prove Gandhi's dreams were shattered by none other than his dearest friends among the Khilafatists – the Ali Brothers.

* * *

Although the Ali Brothers continued their friendship with Gandhi, their attitude towards the Independence movement in general, and Hindu-Muslim unity in particular underwent a sea change. League's attitude towards the Congress began to harden. The country was riled in communal strife in 1922-23. Punjab and Bengal witnessed the worst communal riots in which hundreds were killed, houses looted and burnt and rapes and forced conversions became the order of the day. Amritsar, Lahore, Moradabad, Meerut, Ahmedabad, Bhagalpur, Delhi – many cities with substantial Muslim populations, witnessed rioting.

Kohat was a small town in the North-West Frontier Agency, where a dastardly communal riot broke out in September 1924. The population of Hindus was less than 5 percent in that town among which the majority were killed. A total of 150 deaths of Hindus was reported. Motilal Nehru called it a "tragedy which has not been known in India." "The Muslim fury knew no bounds. Destruction of life and property, in which the constabulary freely partook... was general... Even the Khilafat volunteers, whose duty it was to protect the Hindus, and regard them as their own kith and kin, neglected their duty, and not only joined in the loot, but also took part in the previous incitement," Gandhi himself wrote.[7]

Gandhi wouldn't blame anyone but himself for the Kohat

tragedy. "Had I not been instrumental in bringing into being the vast energy of the people? I must find a remedy if the energy proved self-destructive," he argued.[8]

The remedy was to undertake a twenty-one day fast and the place chosen was the house of Maulana Mohammad Ali. Mohammad Ali had by then become strident in his criticism of Gandhi and had gone back into his pre-1914 mould of Muslim communal politics. But Gandhi's faith in him continued. Mohammad Ali was initially reluctant and argued with Gandhi that if, "he, God forbid, succumbed to the rigorous fast, Hindus would wreak vengeance on Muslims." But Gandhi wouldn't relent. Maulana ensured that regular Quran recitals were arranged during Gandhi's fast.

Not all were happy with Gandhi's decision. When Gandhi was on a tour of the country, a Hindu youth accosted him and asked, "Do you think Hindu-Muslim unity is possible when Maulana Mohammad Ali says that an adulterous Mussalman is superior to Mahatma Gandhi?" Gandhi took pains to explain that the Maulana had not meant it that way. "Maulana's was only a picturesque way of putting it. Why can't you understand such a simple thing? Supposing I have a Kohinoor diamond, and someone says Gandhi is better than a *zamindar* in possessing the Kohinoor diamond, can't he say so? To everyone, his religion is the best in the world, as to every chaste man his wife should be the most beautiful woman in the world. And in the same way Mohammad Ali said, any Mussalman was better than I in having a better creed," he replied[9].

Despite Gandhi's defence, Ali Brothers were changed men after the failure of the Khilafat. They would even level charges of communalism against Gandhi and Motilal Nehru later. In a letter written from his deathbed to British Prime

Minister Ramsay MacDonald, Mohammad Ali wrote in January 1931, that he belonged to "two circles of equal size which are not concentric - one is Indian, and the other is the Muslim world."[10] "We are not nationalists, but super nationalists, and I, as a Muslim, say that God made man and the Devil made nation," he wrote.[11]

This return of stridency was first witnessed in 1923, when the song *Vande Mataram* came in the crosshairs of the Muslim League fanaticism. It became a regular practice since 1905 to sing Bankim Chandra's song of *Vande Mataram* during all the important Congress events. *Modern India*, the textbook authored by historian Bipin Chandra for the NCERT, mentions: "The Partition (of Bengal) took effect on October 16, 1905. The leaders of the movement declared it to be a day of mourning. There was a *hartal* in Calcutta...The streets of Calcutta were full of the cries of *Vande Mataram* which overnight became the national song of Bengal and which was soon to become the theme song of the national movement."

The annual session of the Congress was held at Kakinada in Andhra Pradesh, in December 1923 at a sprawling 120-acre ground provided by the Maharaja of Pithapuram. Thousands of delegates were present at the session. Gandhi was absent as he was incarcerated at Pune's Yerawada Jail. Maulana Mohammad Ali, who was released from prison, was elected as the president of the session. Senior leaders, including Motilal Nehru, Maulana Abul Kalam Azad, Sarojini Naidu, Sardar Patel and Kasturba Gandhi were present along with over twelve thousand delegates.

Like in the past, Pt. Vishnu Digambar Puluskar, a renowned Hindustani musician from Maharashtra, was there to sing Vande Mataram at the inaugural. When Pt. Puluskar climbed the dais to sing , Mohammad Ali raised objection saying that the song would hurt the sentiments of religious Muslims. Seeing the silence of the leaders present on the dais, Puluskar took it upon himself to challenge Mohammad Ali and went ahead with its rendition. "Digambar was incensed and hit back: 'This is a national forum, not the platform of any single community. This is no mosque to object to music. There is no justification for a ban on music here. When the president could put up with the music in the presidential procession, why does he object to it here?' Having silenced the president, without waiting for his reply, he proceeded to sing *Vande Mataram* and completed it. Respect for his sense of national pride and love of the motherland grew. The people admired his moral courage and applauded him heartily," mentions a book on Puluskar about the incident at Kakinada.[12]

Mohammad Ali, in protest, walked away while the song was being sung. It may be worthwhile to mention here that on many earlier occasions, the Ali Brothers and other League leaders used to get up and stand with other Hindu and Muslim members of the Congress, when the song was sung. The objection at the Kakinada session was thus more a part of the enhanced bargaining of the League leadership than a genuinely religious issue.

To placate the League members, the Congress introduced Mohammad Iqbal's famous song '*Saare jahan se acchha – Hindustan Hamara*' in its sessions a couple of years before. Yet, the opposition to *Vande Mataram* continued. It became a part of the so-called 'Muslim grievances' against the Congress.

In July 1939, Gandhi wrote in *Harijan* that Vande Mataram, "no matter what its source was, and how and when it was composed, had become a most powerful battle-cry among Hindus and Musalmans of Bengal during the Partition days. It was an anti-imperialist cry. As a lad, when I knew nothing of *Anandmath* or even Bankim, its immortal author, *Vande Mataram* had gripped me and when I first heard it sung, it had enthralled me. I associated the purest national spirit with it. It never occurred to me that it was a Hindu song or meant only for Hindus. Unfortunately, now we have fallen on evil days..."[13]

But the League's insistence on rejecting it had a dramatic impact. In 1937, when the elections were held to the Provincial Councils, the Congress formed governments in several of them. When the Congress leadership initiated a dialogue with Jinnah, who by then had become the supreme leader of the Muslim League, to form coalition governments, Jinnah invoked the grievance of the League about *Vande Mataram* and insisted that the song cannot be sung at the commencement of the sessions. A committee was hurriedly constituted by the Congress to review *Vande Mataram*. Rabindranath Tagore, Subhas Chandra Bose and Jawaharlal Nehru were made its members. The committee recommended to the Congress Working Committee that the song be truncated and only the first two stanzas be sung.

The national song was truncated in 1937 to appease the Muslim League. Ten years later, the nation was partitioned.

* * *

The Muslim League's grievances were not confined to *Vande Mataram* song alone. The League was opposed to the Indian national flag too.

In 1921, Gandhi himself proposed in an article in *Harijan* that the freedom movement should have a flag.

Pingali Venkaiah, a young Congress activist from Andhra, had been proposing several designs for many years for the same. Gandhi asked him to come up with a proper national flag to be adopted by the Congress at its session in Bezawada (Vijayawada), in Andhra Pradesh, in 1921. Venkaiah came up with the suggestion of a flag with two colours – saffron and green – representing Hindus and Muslims, with a *charkha* – spinning wheel in the middle. Gandhi liked it but recommended that white also be added to represent the other communities. Since then, the tricolour flag became a part of the Congress movement.

However, at the Karachi Congress session in 1931, a formal Flag Committee was constituted to recommend the future national flag of Independent India. Pattabhi Sitaramaiah was its convenor, while Sardar Vallabhbhai Patel, Jawaharlal Nehru, Abul Kalam Azad, Master Tara Singh and Kaka Kalelkar were made the members. The committee met a few times and studied various designs. In its recommendations submitted to the Working Committee, the Flag Committee unanimously opined that '*kesari* colour' (saffron colour) flag should be adopted.

"We feel the flag must be distinctive, artistic, rectangular and non-communal. Opinion has been unanimous that our national flag should be of a single colour, except for the colour of the device. If there is one colour, that is more acceptable to the Indians as a whole, even as it is more distinctive than another; one that is associated with this ancient country by long tradition, it is the *kesari* or saffron colour. Accordingly, it is felt that the flag should be of the *kesari* colour, except for the colour of the device. That the device should be the *charkha* is unanimously agreed too. Various other devices have been suggested in place of or in addition to the *charkha*–

namely plough, lotus flower and so on. But the *charkha* is really the device around which our national movement has grown these ten years, and its importance should not be lessened by the addition of any other device. We have then to select the colour of the device. The Committee has come to the conclusion that the *charkha* should be in blue. Accordingly, we recommend that the national flag should be of *kesari* or saffron colour, having on it at the left top quarter the *charkha* in blue with the wheel towards the flagstaff, the proportions of the flag being fly to hoist as three to two," the Committee wrote.[14]

But the Congress leadership was concerned about the reaction of the Muslim League. It was decided that the tricolour flag, which was in vogue for the last decade or so, would continue to be used. Initially, even Gandhi used to identify the three colours with different religions of India. But later, the description was modified to make it more egalitarian. Eminent scholar of Hinduism, Dr. Sarvepalli Radhakrishnan, who became the Vice President of Independent India, explained the significance of the three colours later as: "*Bhagwa* or the saffron denotes renunciation or disinterestedness. Our leaders must be indifferent to material gains and dedicate themselves to their work. The white in the centre is light, the path of truth to guide our conduct. The green shows our relation to (the) soil, our relation to the plant life here, on which all other life depends. The 'Ashoka *chakra*' in the centre of the white is the wheel of the law of *dharma*. Truth or *satya*, *dharma* or virtue, ought to be the controlling principle of those who work under this flag. Again, the wheel denotes motion. There is death in stagnation. There is life in movement. India should no more resist change; it must move and go forward.

The wheel represents the dynamism of a peaceful change."[15]

* * *

The compromises galore of the Congress leadership continued with the avowed objective of keeping the Muslim League on their side. When some League leaders projected Hindi as the language of the Hindus, Congress passed a resolution suggesting that Hindustani, a hybrid product of the mixture of Hindi and Urdu, would be accepted as the national language, irrespective of whether the script was Nagri or Urdu. Hindustani came to be used increasingly in the Congress literature.

Gandhi modified Hindu *bhajans*, like '*Raghupati Raghav Rajaram*' to add '*Ishvar-Allah tere naam*'. Poet Bhushan's *Shiv Bavni*, a compilation of 52 stanzas praising Shivaji Maharaj, used to be popular among the Hindus in those days. It was generally discouraged as it had the potential to offend the Muslims.

Then came the most contentious question of cow-slaughter. At the height of the Hindu-Muslim bonhomie during the Khilafat movement, when some Muslim leaders like Maulana Abdul Bari called upon Muslims to give up cow slaughter and refrain from eating beef as a gesture of goodwill towards Hindus, Gandhi took the principled stand that it should not become a bargaining deal. "Muslims should not give up slaughtering it only to appease the Hindus. They should be convinced that the Hindu sentiment about the cow has a certain logic and sanctity behind it. Muslims should respect their feelings out of conviction," he insisted.[16]

But later, as the Muslim separatism grew and so did the demands of the League leadership, Congress would change its stance to keep the League followers in good humour. As

Jinnah was upping the ante against the Congress on all and sundry issues, the jittery Congress leadership would bend backwards to 'reassure' him about their sincerity. In a letter to Jinnah in 1938, Nehru said that there had "been a great deal of entirely false and unfounded propaganda against the Congress suggesting that the Congress was going to stop [cow-slaughter] forcibly by legislation."[17] He assured Jinnah that the Congress did "not wish to undertake any legislative action in this matter to restrict the established rights of the Muslims."[18] Nehru or no other Congress leader had ever explained as to how and when the killing of cows became the 'established right' of the Muslims.

Confronted by constant appeals from the Hindu masses, Gandhi would turn his helplessness into anguish and anger against those who demanded a ban on cow-slaughter. At a prayer meeting on July 25, 1947, days before the Partition holocaust was to begin, Gandhi would chide his followers from sending him thousands of telegrams demanding ban on cow-slaughter:

"Rajendra Babu tells me that he has received some 50,000 postcards, between 25,000 and 30,000 letters and many thousands of telegrams demanding a ban on cow-slaughter. I spoke to you about this before. Why this flood of telegrams and letters? They have had no effect.We have been shouting from the house-tops that there will be no coercion in the matter of religion. We have been reciting verses from the Koran at the prayer. But if anyone were to force me to recite these verses, I would not like it. How can I force anyone not to slaughter cows unless he is himself so disposed? It is not as if there were only Hindus in the Indian Union. There are Muslims, Parsees, Christians and other religious groups here.

"Besides some prosperous Hindus themselves encourage cow-slaughter. True, they do not do it with their own hands. But who sends all the cows to Australia and other countries where they are slaughtered and whence shoes manufactured from cow hide are sent back to India? I know an orthodox Vaishnav Hindu. He used to feed his children on beef soup. On my asking him why he did that, he said there was no sin in consuming beef as medicine".[19]

* * *

As the Congress' politics of appeasement reached unreasonable proportions, another ghastly incident happened - the gory murder of Swami Shraddhananda. Shraddhanad was an Arya Samaj leader, who was active in Congress politics too since the time of the Khilafat and non-cooperation movement. Standing on the steps of Delhi's famed Jama Masjid in 1920, Shraddhananda had exhorted Muslims to unitedly fight for Independence together with Hindus. He also actively participated in the Khilafat movement.

But the fallout of the Khilafat movement and growing atrocities against the Hindus had motivated Shraddhananda to return to the Hindu reformist movement after 1923. He resumed his Swami Dayanand-inspired Arya Samaj movement for *shuddhi* of converted Hindus and brought thousands of them back into the Hindu fold. He was also engaged in ending social evils within the Hindu society, like untouchability and caste discrimination, for which Dr. Ambedkar praised him as "the greatest and most sincere champion of the untouchables".[20]

Shraddhananda focused his efforts on the *shuddhi* of the Malkana Rajputs in western parts of the United Provinces.

These Rajputs were Hindus but used to follow many Muslim practices. Upon their own urging, Shraddhanad undertook their *shuddhi* programme. It angered many Muslim clerics of that region. Fanatic Muslim elements started looking at Shraddhananda's Hindu reformist movement as a challenge to Islam.

On December 23, 1926, Shraddhananda had returned from a long trip and retired into his room at the Naya Bazar in Delhi, for rest. He suffered from a deadly attack of pneumonia and was advised rest. At around 4 p.m. that evening, a Muslim man entered his house and insisted on having a word with him. Dharam Singh, the attendant explained to him that the Swami was unwell, but the Swami heard the conversation and allowed the young man to come into his room. As Dharam Singh moved out of the room to fetch some water, Abdul Rashid, the Muslim fanatic whipped out a revolver and pumped bullets into Swami Shraddhanand's 70-year-old body from a point-blank range. Shraddhananda died instantly.

The entire nation was shocked at the brutality of the murder of a Hindu saint, who was, until a few years ago, rubbing shoulders with the very same Muslims, whose cause of Khilafat he also championed.

The annual Congress session took place at Guwahati at that time. News of Shraddhananda's murder reached there. Gandhi too was shocked and condemned the dastardly act, but he refused to blame Rashid. He instead blamed those who created an atmosphere of hatred "where someone would lose his balance and resort to such an inhuman act." The fault, according to him, was not that of Rashid, but it lay at the doors of everyone who had poisoned the atmosphere, that included Swami Shraddhananda himself. He singled out the media-men, who, of late, had become “a walking plague”.

Gandhi indulged in strange arguments. “It is we, the educated and semi-educated class that are responsible for the hot fever that possessed Abdul Rashid. It is unnecessary to discriminate and apportion the share of blame between two rival parties,” he argued. “Today it is a Mussalman who has murdered a Hindu. We should not be surprised if a Hindu killed a Mussalman. God forbid that this should happen but what else can one expect when we cannot control our tongue or our pen?” he contended.[21]

Gandhi’s reference to Abdul Rashid as a ‘dear brother’ had ruffled the feathers of many in the crowd. Gandhi made more comments on December 26. “Brother Abdul Rashid was shown in. I purposely call him brother, and if we are true Hindus, you will understand why I call him so,” he said on that day.[22]

“Now you will, perhaps, understand why I have called Abdul Rashid a brother, and I repeat it, I do not even regard him as guilty of Swami’s murder. Guilty, indeed, are all those who excited feelings of hatred against one another,” Gandhi reiterated.[23]

A few days later, on December 30, Gandhi wrote in *Young India*: “I wish to plead for Abdul Rashid. I do not know who he is. It does not matter to me what prompted the deed. The fault is ours.”[24]

The obsession had reached maddening proportions. One man, who watched it closely and exploited it fully was Mohammad Ali Jinnah.

Reference—

1. *Nanda, B.R. (1989), "Gandhi: Pan-Islamism, Imperialism and Nationalism In India" p. 345, Oxford University Press, Delhi*
2. *Rajagopalachari, C. (1922), "Jail Diary" p. 102*
3. *Nanda, B.R. (1989), "Gandhi: Pan-Islamism, Imperialism and Nationalism In India" p. 359, Oxford University Press, Delhi*
4. *Lewis, Bernard (1961), "The Emergence of Modern Turkey" pp. 263, Oxford University Press, London*
5. *Nanda, B.R. (1989), "Gandhi: Pan-Islamism, Imperialism and Nationalism In India" p. 366, Oxford University Press, Delhi*
6. *Nanda, B.R. (1989), "Gandhi: Pan-Islamism, Imperialism and Nationalism In India" p. 357, Oxford University Press, Delhi*
7. *Majumdar, R.C. (1964), "History of the Freedom Movements in India: Vol.-III" p. 279, Firma K.L. Mukhopadhyay*
8. *Balakrishna, Sandeep, "How Kohat was Entirely Cleansed of its Hindu Population: The Tragic Finale" accessed at https://www.dharmadispatch.in/history/how-kohat-was-entirely-cleansed-of-its-hindu-population-the-tragic-finale*
9. *Tendulkar, D.G. (1951-54), "Mahatama" Vol. II, pp. 252, Greenleaf Books*
10. *Minault, Gail (1982), "The Khilafat Movement: Religious Symbolism and Political Mobilisation in India" p. 237, New York Columbia University Press*
11. *Nanda, B.R. (1989), "Gandhi: Pan-Islamism, Imperialism and Nationalism In India" p. 390, Oxford University Press, Delhi*
12. *"Vishnu Digambar Paluskar" p. 54, National Book Trust*
13. *Gandhi, M.K. (July 1, 1939), "Harijan: Vol-VII, p. 21"*
14. *"Report of the National Flag Committee" p. 4, Indian National Congress, 1931*
15. *"Flag Code of India 2002" Ministry of Home Affairs, Government of India*
16. *Zakaria, Rafiq (1999), "Gandhi and the Break-Up of India" pp. 48, Bharatiya Vidya Bhavan*
17. *"Selected Works of Jawaharlal Nehru: Vol. Eight" p. 236, Hind Swaraj, B.R. Publishing Company, 1972*
18. *Ibid.*
19. *"PrarthanaPravacjan: Part I" p. 277-280*
20. *"Dr. B.R. Ambedkar: Writngs and Speeches: Vol.-IX" p. 23-24, Dr. Ambedkar Foundation, 1991*
21. *"Collected Works of Mahatama Gandhi: Vol-37" p. 434-437, Gandhi Sevagram Ashram*

22. *Ibid.*
23. *Ibid.*
24. *"Collected Works of Mahatama Gandhi: Vol-37" p. 457, Gandhi Sevagram Ashram*

□

Two Mistakes of Congress Jinnah's Revival

There is no power on earth that can undo Pakistan.
—Jinnah

A decade of appeasement and compromise on the part of the Congress leadership only led to the further hardening of the Muslim League's attitude. Instead of bringing Hindus and Muslims closer, it only helped in further fortifying separate identities. By the 1930s, leaders of the League, like Jinnah and Aga Khan, started insisting that the League was the sole representative of Muslims in India. That "Hindus and Muslims are two distinct races" became the more dominant theme instead of the coveted "Hindu-Muslim unity". It would eventually lead to the birth of the infamous "Two-Nation Theory", which Jinnah flaunted in late 1930s and through the 1940s until he achieved his goal of the Partition of India and creation of a Muslim State, called Pakistan.

Simon Commission came to India in 1928 to study the constitutional reforms needed for the country and challenged the Congress leadership to prepare its own constitution for India. The leadership accepted that challenge and formed an All-Parties Conference under the leadership of Motilal

Nehru for that task. The draft report, which came to be known as the "Nehru Report", was soon ready in which four important demands were made. Main demand of the Nehru Report was Dominion Status on par with Canada under the British suzerainty. It had many other domestic proposals which were subsequently incorporated in the constitution of independent India.

Nehru Report completely ignored League demands. As a result, the League leadership rejected it. It continued its demand for separate electorates and "weighted representation". Jinnah came out with a charter of fourteen demands that included one-third representation of Muslims in central legislature and reasonable share for Muslims in government jobs and preferment.

By then, Gandhi and the other Congress leaders were so disenchanted with the Muslim League leadership that the talk of Hindu-Muslim unity lost all its steam in the country. The League leadership had used every forum including the Round Table Conferences to push ahead with their unending demands. Miffed with this attitude, Nehru shot off a letter to Gandhi. "If I had to listen to my dear friend Mohammad Ali Jinnah talking the most unmitigated nonsense about his 14 points for any length of time, I would have to consider the desirability of retiring to the South Sea islands, where there would be some hope of meeting with some people who were intelligent or ignorant enough not to talk of the 14 points. I marvel at your patience," he wrote with biting sarcasm.[1]

League leaders also engaged in the mischief of hobnobbing with other smaller groups, like the Sikh and Scheduled Caste representatives in order to further embarrass the Congress leadership. The three Round Table

Conferences, held in succession during 1930-32, ended as a failure for the Congress precisely due to this attitude and machinations of the League leadership.

Congress had generally kept away from Round Table Conferences. Gandhi was the sole representative present in the second conference held in September 1931. League leadership played a more divisive role. Jinnah and Agha Khan represented the League in London for the conference. Dr. B.R. Ambedkar was there, representing the Depressed Classes. There were representatives from Sikh, Buddhist, Anglo-Indian and princely states groups. Behind Gandhi's back, Agha Khan held secret meetings with the leaders of various groups and put forward a proposal before the British for enhanced separate representation for all these groups in the Indian legislature. Gandhi firmly rejected further fragmentation of the Indian society in the name of separate electorates.

On the issue of separate electorates for 'Untouchables', as they were called at that time, Gandhi was uncompromising. "I can understand the claims advanced by other minorities, but the claims advanced on behalf of the Untouchables is to me the unkindest cut of all. It means perpetual bar sinister. We do not want on our register and on our Census Untouchables classified as a separate class. Sikhs may remain as such in perpetuity, so may Muslims, so may Europeans. Would Untouchables remain in perpetuity? I would far rather that Hinduism died than that Untouchability lived," he thundered.[2]

The British Prime Minister Ramsay McDonald went ahead with a modified version of the League's recommendations and announced the famous Communal Award 1932. It came as a rude shock to the Congress leadership. They were especially aghast at the British decision to provide exclusive electorates for the Depressed Classes by separating them from the Hindus.

Gandhi viewed the Communal Award as the negation of his years of toil. He believed rightly that separate electorates for depressed classes would eventually perpetuate social evils like Untouchability as they exclude those classes from the rest of Hindu society. Disheartened and back in India, Gandhi announced an indefinite fast against the Award on September 20, 1932.

Congress leadership persuaded the leader of the depressed classes, Dr. B.R. Ambedkar for negotiations with Gandhi at the Yerawada prison. The negotiations led to the Poona Pact, which was signed by Dr. Ambedkar and Madan Mohan Malviya. Under the pact, Dr. Ambedkar had agreed to give up the demand for exclusive electorates for the depressed classes, and secured instead, enhanced number of seats for the community from 71 to 147 under the Hindu quota of the seats. The Communal Award was accordingly amended in 1933. Gandhi could thus prevent Hindu society from further fragmentation.

Gandhi was particularly upset with the League's mischief at promoting more divisions within the Indian society and told Mohammad Iqbal, who was a prominent member from the League besides Aga Khan and Jinnah, that any further discussion about their demands was possible only when they give up their mischief of encouraging further fragmentation of the Indian society. But Iqbal insisted that their claims were akin to the claims of Untouchables, and hence he cannot but support them.

Meanwhile, competitive minorityism had reached the doorsteps of the Congress also with the Muslim leaders in Congress openly supporting the Communal Award. Though opposed to the Communal Award in principle, the Congress was put in a tight spot due to this. Finally, it took a bizarre stand of "neither accepting nor rejecting" the Communal Award. This stand of the Congress irked leaders like Madan Mohan Malviya and Loknayak Ane, who resigned and started the Congress Nationalist Party.

The Communal Award came as a major setback to Gandhi's efforts for Hindu-Muslim unity and gave greater teeth to Jinnah and the Muslim League. Jinnah started insisting more vociferously that the Congress should represent Hindus only. The stridency of the League's separatist rhetoric too increased.

Gandhi started feeling that Congress was no longer the place to pursue his agenda. Conditions that led to the Puna Pact compelled him to think of devoting more time to the Harijan work. By then, Jawaharlal rose to occupy a prominent position within the Congress organization. Nehru, with his Marxist sensibilities could not understand Gandhi's emphasis on social unity and personal purification. For him, everything was political or economic. As the gap between the two started growing, Gandhi came to the view that he was unwelcome for the intellectual leadership of the Congress. Although younger sections of the Congress were attracted by Gandhi's program, he was generally disillusioned with the functioning of the organization. He also received many reports of corruption in the Congress units. He decided in 1934 to resign from the membership of the Congress.

"In 1922, he had come to believe that Indians were not

yet worthy of swaraj; by 1934 he had come to suspect that the Congress was not fit to govern", comments Roderick Matthews.[3]

* * *

In August 1935, the British Government promulgated the Government of India Act under which greater autonomy was given to the Provincial Councils. Reorganisation of provinces also took place, and more than thirty-five million people were given the right of franchise. Elections were announced to the Provincial Councils in 1937.

The Congress decided to plunge into elections. Since Gandhi had resigned from the membership of the Congress after the Round Table experience, the responsibility for electioneering was completely on the shoulders of Nehru, while Patel, Rajendra Prasad and Abul Kalam Azad were handling party affairs.

Muslim League was rudderless as Jinnah decided to stay back in London after the Round Table Conferences and continue his lucrative practice at the Privy Council. He even confessed to an Indian journalist that "I seem to have reached a dead end"[4]. Jinnah's absence left the League in a disarray. Several smaller regional Muslim outfits with considerable local influences sprouted up in different provinces. But when elections were announced, Jinnah decided to come back and rejuvenate the League.

Matters were not easy for Jinnah. When he visited Punjab in 1936, Jinnah "got the political equivalent of a bloody nose"[5]. Muslims of Punjab shunned him publicly and privately. While the senior leader of the Unionist Party, Fazl-i-Hussain noted in his diary that Jinnah was "no leader", Jinnah himself called Punjab a "hopeless place"[6].

Rattled by the rejection of Muslims to his overtures, Jinnah approached Gandhi with a proposal for reconciliation, but Gandhi was, by then, out of the organisational politics of the Congress and hence, advised Jinnah to talk to Nehru or Prasad. Jinnah made a public statement suggesting that he would be open to extending Muslim League's support to Congress after the elections. Nehru was never positive about Jinnah. When he heard about Jinnah's overtures, Nehru mocked at him and said, "I thank Mr. Jinnah for the offer. But so far as our fight for freedom is concerned, it is going to be carried on by the Indian National Congress alone"[7]. He categorically declared that there were only two parties to the Independence struggle – The British and the Congress. A miffed Jinnah retorted, saying, "No, there is the third one – the Muslims".

A bigger shock awaited Jinnah in the provincial elections next year.

The provincial elections of 1937 provided an excellent opportunity to the Congress. Despite its separatist rhetoric, the Muslim League was decisively rejected in all Muslim provinces of the country. Out of the 482 exclusive Muslim constituencies, the League could hardly win 109 seats. While the Congress could form governments in eight of the eleven provinces, the League couldn't form even in one. In Bengal, it managed a coalition with Fazlul Haq's Krishak Praja Party. Congress secured majorities in all Hindu majority provinces – Bombay, Madras, the Central Provinces, Bihar, Orissa (last two were carved out of Bengal under the 1935 Act). In Assam, a third province carved out in 1935, League was trounced by a local party called the Assam Valley Muslim Party. The province too eventually went into Congress kitty a year later in 1938. In the United Provinces, where there was a large Muslim electorate, the Muslim landlords tried their best to stall the Congress. Yet, the results went in Congress' favour finally. Congress registered a big win in the Muslim province of NWFP, where the Pathan strongmen Khan Abdul Gaffar Khan, later came to be known as 'Frontier Gandhi', and his elder brother Khan Abdul Jabbar Khan made sure that League doesn't secure any foothold.

Muslim voters preferred other regional Muslim parties like the Unionists led by Fazl-i-Hussain in Punjab and Krishak Praja Party led by Fazlul Haq in Bengal Victory eluded League even in Sindh, where the electorate delivered a fractured mandate with All India Muslim Conference, an anti-Jinnah alliance taking lead in forming the government. In the final tally, in 1937, Muslim League's support at the national level was reduced to as low as 5%. Far from being a national party, Jinnah's party was no longer even a party that the Muslims supported.

Jinnah was desperate and decided to up his ante against Gandhi and Congress. He was convinced that an all-out attack was the only option left for him to wean away the Muslims from the Congress and parties sympathetic to it. He received a letter from his old acquaintance Sir Muhammad Iqbal in May 1937 in which Iqbal cautioned that the Muslim masses were not showing interest in the politics of the League because they saw it as a party of the upper classes and landlords. He advised Jinnah to appeal to the Muslim masses in the name of "the law of Islam"[8]. Thereafter Jinnah's single-minded focus was to win back Muslim support for the League. He launched a virulent campaign, propagating that the Congress would usher in an oppressive 'Hindu Raj', in which Muslims would be slave citizens. He was himself never a practicing Muslim, yet he gave the call of 'Islam in danger' to attract Muslims.

It was around this time, in October 1937, that Jinnah started wearing Sherwani. At a conference in Allahabad in January 1938, he even called himself a "proud communalist". He also started imitating Congress in organisational affairs of the League. A new structure was given to the League from top to bottom. Jinnah was clear that like Congress, League too should acquire the stature of a mass movement by shedding its elitist character.

At this juncture, two steps taken by the Congress leadership helped Jinnah revive his fortunes once again. First was Gandhi's decision to reach out to Jinnah for a compromise. Gandhi was disturbed by Jinnah's rhetoric and feared that it would lead to Muslims gravitating towards Jinnah and League. As a moralist, that would have been a death knell to his dream of Hindu-Muslim unity. In February, he decided to write a letter to Jinnah.

In that letter, Gandhi tried to pander to Jinnah by invoking his nationalist past. "In your speeches I miss the old nationalist. When in 1915, I returned from my self-imposed exile in South Africa, everybody spoke of you as one of the staunchest nationalists and the hope of both Hindus and Mussalmans. Are you still the same Jinnah? If you say you are, in spite of your speeches, I shall accept your word," he wrote.[9]

Jinnah seized the opportunity for grandstanding and told Gandhi bluntly, "You recognise All-India Muslim League as the one authoritative and representative organisation of the Mussalmans of India and on the other hand, you represent the Congress and other Hindus throughout the country. It is only on that basis we can proceed further and further devise a machinery for approach."[10]

Despite this rebuff, Gandhi decided to meet Jinnah in person. The meeting took place on April 28, 1938, at Jinnah's residence in Bombay. Nothing was to come out of the meeting, given Jinnah's attitude. Nothing came out too. Jinnah stuck to his arguments – Gandhi should agree that he was the leader of the Hindus and Jinnah should be accepted as the undisputed leader of the Muslims; the Congress should consider itself as a party of the Hindus and League should be recognised as the representative of Muslims. And finally, Gandhi should not quibble about the Two-Nation Theory and realise that a solution was possible only on that basis.

Gandhi-Jinnah talks didn't yield any results – neither for Gandhi nor the Congress, but they enhanced the stature of Jinnah in the eyes of the Muslims considerably. These talks were followed by an exchange of letters between Nehru and Jinnah. Nehru agreed for correspondence out of his respect for Gandhi, but he refused to respond to Jinnah's substantive points. In the end, the correspondence only led to further deterioration of the relationship.

It was the turn of Subhash. As the newly elected President of Congress, Subahsh Bose opened dialogue with Jinnah. That correspondence too did not yield any result. Jinnah was immovable. He wrote to Gandhi demanding strangely that no Muslim should be appointed to Congress committees without his consent. At the same time, he approached the Viceroy offering his services to the British if they agree to recognize him as the sole voice of the Muslims. Two deacdes ago Jinnah would abhor any such suggestion. But now he was ready to support the British.

At the League Conference in Patna in December 1938, Jinnah made a vitriolic attack on Congress and Gandhi. He called Congress as nothing but a Hindu body, and blamed Gandhi for trying to establish Hindu Raj in India. Two decades ago, he conveyed his opposition to Gandhi's mass politics saying politics should be a 'gentlemen's business'. But at Patna, he said that politics should be played "as on a chessboard"[11].

Rafiq Zakaria succinctly points out the difference in attitudes of Gandhi and Jinnah. "The Ali Brothers, with all their faults, believed in give and take. Jinnah, on the other hand, refused to budge from the stand he took. He was more a lawyer than a leader. He was a stickler for technicalities. Gandhi was made differently. He believed in compromise and worked for it. Jinnah was never known to opt for a compromise even at the bar. His aim was to succeed. It was victory that mattered, not the merits or the demerits of a case. His outlook remained the same in politics. He and Gandhi were two odd men".[12]

The second mistake by the Congress that helped 'odd man' Jinnah was the decision to ask provincial governments to resign on October 22, 1939, on the issue of Viceroy Linlithgow's unilateral move to involve India in the Second World War without committing to grant self-rule after the war. League seized this opportunity and declared its support to the British in return for enhanced protection to the League in provinces. Jinnah appealed to the Muslims to celebrate December 22, 1939, as the 'Day of Deliverance' from the 'anti-Muslim Congress regime'. A few months earlier, Jinnah appointed a committee under the leadership of Raja Saheb of

Pirpur to investigate into the purported atrocities committed by the Congress governments against Muslims. Replete with exaggerations and lies, that report was released at the end of October that year and was used as a propaganda material during the events on the 'Day of Deliverance'.

A resolution was passed by the League units across the country. "The Congress governments constantly interfered with the legitimate and routine duties of district officers even in petty matters to the serious detriment of the Mussalmans and thereby created an atmosphere which spread the belief amongst the Hindu public that there was established a Hindu Raj, and emboldened the Hindus, mostly Congressmen, to ill-treat Muslims at various places and interfere with their elementary rights of freedom. Therefore, it expresses its deep sense of relief at the termination of the Congress regime in various provinces and rejoices in observing this day as the 'Day of Deliverance' from tyranny, oppression and injustice during the last two-and-a-half years, and prays to God to grant such strength, discipline and organisation to Muslim India as to successfully prevent the advent of such a ministry again and to establish a truly popular ministry, which would do even justice to all communities and interests," the resolution read.[13]

It was clear from the resolution that Jinnah had become adamant and hell bent on opposing any and every move of the Congress. He would use his legal acumen to twist and distort whatever Gandhi or Congress said and accused them of injustice. Once Gandhi affectionately referred to him as 'Brother Jinnah', and Jinnah rebutted, saying, "Brother Gandhi forgets that he has three votes and I have one." When Gandhi called Partition a sin, Jinnah went to town, misleadingly telling Muslims, "Gandhi has called your demand a sin, not even a crime. He has damned you in this world as well as the next."

Dawn, the paper he started to promote the Muslim League's agenda, started spewing venom through exaggerated claims and lies. It ran a thirty-two-part series on the supposed "holocaust" being perpetrated by Congress against Muslims. Across India, "tragedy followed tragedy and blood flowed instead of the milk of kindness. Terror stalked the countryside and rendered the helpless, outnumbered few despairing and desperate", it claimed[14].

Jinnah, who once blamed Gandhi for mixing up religion with politics, now started blatantly resorting to communal appeals. League flyers in the elections were full of religious symbolism assuring Muslim voters that God and the Prophet favoured the League's candidates.The British governor of Punjab, Sir Bertrand Glancy, predicted that "The uninformed Muslim will be told that the question he is called on to answer at the polls is – 'Are you a true believer or an infidel and a traitor?'" One Mullah in Punjab warned that any Muslims who did not vote for the League and Pakistan would be "fuel for the fires of Hell". Many Sufi saints issued fatwas saying that the "Muslim League is the only Islamic community and... all the rest are kafirs"[15].

"Everything was fair for Jinnah in his fight against Gandhi," wryly observes Rafiq.[16]

* * *

In their eagerness to prove that the Congress represented all the Indians, Congress leaders used the annual session in December 1938 to equate Muslim League with Hindu Mahasabha and branded both as communal bodies. Jinnah hit back, saying that it was the Congress which had represented Hindus and the League was the sole representative of the Muslims. The next couple of years saw the relations on a steep downward slide. Finally, Jinnah declared that he wouldn't have anything to do with Congress anymore until and unless it conceded that League was the sole representative of Indian Muslims.

Congress' misstep in quitting from the provincial governments had another unintended effect. It left the smaller regional parties that were banking on Congress' support, weak and helpless. Jinnah quickly stepped in and used his diplomatic and persuasive skills to win over some of these regional Muslim leaders to the League's side. Prominent among those who joined Jinnah during those critical years included Sir Sikandar Hayat Khan, the premier of Punjab; Fazlul Haq, the Premier of Bengal; and Sir M. Sadullah, the Assam Premier.

The British too found an opportunity to fish in troubled waters with this Congress-League quarrel. Viceroy Linlithgow reassured Jinnah that "His Majesty's government recognised the fact that the All-India Muslim League alone truly represents the Muslims of India and can speak on their behalf."[17] While the Congress was crestfallen, it helped boost Jinnah's prospects, including winning over the remaining Muslim leaders to his side.

It is under these circumstances, when the Congress was on the backfoot and the League on the ascendancy, that Jinnah called the Muslim League session at Lahore in March 1940. It was in this session that the famous resolution for Pakistan was unanimously passed by the Muslim League for the first time. Eleven years before , at the very site in Lahore, the Congress, under the leadership of Jawaharlal

Nehru, had passed the resolution demanding *purna swaraj* – total Independence. Eleven years later, the same venue was witness to India being prepared for its Partition.

With Mohammad Iqbal, the first architect of the idea of a separate Muslim State dead, it was Jinnah all the way at the Lahore session. He was determined to achieve his goal by hook or by crook. He presented his scheme for Partition under which the Hindu-majority areas were to become India and the Muslim-majority areas were to become a separate Muslim nation. Referring to his pet theory that Hindus and Muslims were two distinct nations, Jinnah argued in his presidential address: "Islam and Hinduism are not religions in the strict sense of the word, but are, in fact, different and distinct social orders and it is only a dream that the Hindus and the Muslims can ever evolve a common nationality... Muslims are a nation, according to any definition of a nation and they must have their homeland, their territory and their State".[18]

This was the first categorical assertion about the Two-Nation Theory. Some Muslims in Sindh and elsewhere opposed it but their voices were too feeble. Maulana Azad, as the president of the Congress, had spiritedly negated Jinnah's line of argument, but Jinnah simply dismissed him as a Congress 'show boy', and asked him to 'shut up'. For some reason, other than making a statement, Azad didn't make any special efforts to mobilise Muslims in Congress' favour.

Naturally, the only staunch voice of conviction against Jinnah's Two-Nation Theory was that of Gandhi's. "The Two-Nation Theory is an untruth. The vast majority of Muslims of India are converts to Islam or are the descendants of converts. They did not become a separate nation as soon as they became converts. A Bengali Muslim speaks the same tongue that a Bengali Hindu does, eats the same food and has the same amusements as his Hindu neighbour. They dress alike. I have often found it difficult to distinguish by outward sign, between a Bengali Hindu and a Bengali Muslim. The same phenomenon is observable more or less in the South among the poor, who constitute the masses of India," Gandhi said.[19]

"I must rebel against the idea that millions of Indians who were Hindus the other day changed their nationality on adopting Islam as their religion," he vainly argued.[20] He could clearly see his life's work of Hindu-Muslim unity being dismantled by the crude machinations of a man who was hardly a believing Muslim. He was desperate. "To divide it (India) into two is worse than anarchy. It is vivisection which cannot be tolerated,"[21] he cried out and poured out his anguish finally, saying "vivisect me before you vivisect India".

It was too late. Gandhi admitted that 'separate electorates', which the Congress had enthusiastically supported two decades before, were the main reason for "the separation of hearts", but the two decades of appeasement and pandering to these separatist sentiments had now reached the country to a point of no return.

Reference—

1. *Zakaria, Rafiq (1999), "Gandhi and the Break-Up of India" p. 119, Bharatiya Vidya Bhavan*
2. *Ambedkar, B.R. (1945), "What Congress and Gandhi have done to the Untouchables" p. 68, Thacker and Co., Bombay*
3. *Matthews, Roderick "Jinnah vs Gandhi" pp. 133, Hachette India*
4. *Das, Durga (1970), "India: From Curzon to Nehru and After" pp. 155, Collins, London*

5. *Matthews, Roderick "Jinnah vs Gandhi" pp. 137, Hachette India*
6. *Jalal, Ayesha (1994) "The Sole Spokesman: Jinnah, The Muslim League and The Demand for Pakistan" pp.22, CambridgeUniversity Press*
7. *Hajari, Nisid (2015), "Midnight's Furies: The Deadly Legacy of India's Partition" pp. 42, Houghton Mifflin Harcourt*
8. *Jalal, Ayesha (1994) "The Sole Spokesman: Jinnah, The Muslim League and The Demand for Pakistan" pp. 42, Cambridge University Press*
9. *"Famous Letters of Mahatama Gandhi" p. 108-09 accessed at https://www.mkgandhi.org/selectedletters/74majinnah.html*
10. *Prasad, Rajendra (1947), "India Divided" p. 154, Hind Kitab Ltd*
11. *Matthews, Roderick "Jinnah vs Gandhi" pp. 145, Hachette India*
12. *Zakaria, Rafiq (1999), "Gandhi and the Break-Up of India" p. 152, Bharatiya Vidya Bhavan*
13. *Mishra, Vibhuti Bhushan (1987), "Evolution of the Constitutional History of India: 1773-1947" p. 225, Mittal Publications*
14. *Hajari, Nisid (2015), "Midnight's Furies: The Deadly Legacy of India's Partition" pp. 44, Houghton Mifflin Harcourt*
15. *Hajari, Nisid (2015), "Midnight's Furies: The Deadly Legacy of India's Partition" pp. 52, Houghton Mifflin Harcourt*
16. *Zakaria, Rafiq (1999), "Gandhi and the Break-Up of India" p. 156-157, Bharatiya Vidya Bhavan*
17. *Jalal, Ayesha (1985) "The Sole Spokesman: Jinnah, the Muslim League and the Demand for Pakistan" p. 48, Cambridge University Press, Great Britain*
18. *"Address by Quaid-i-Azam Mohammad Ali Jinnah at Lahore Session of Muslim League" p. 5-23, Directorate of Films and Publishing, Ministry of Information and Broadcasting, Government of Pakistan, March 1940*
19. *Gandhi, M.K. (April 6, 1940), "Harijan: Vol.-VIII, p. 8"*
20. *Gandhi, M.K. (1947), "India of my Dreams" p. VI, Navajivan Publishing House, Ahmedabad*
21. *Gandhi, M.K. (September 22, 1940), "Harijan: Vol.-VIII, p. 32"*

□

Separate Electorates To Separate Nations

I find no parallel in history for a body of converts and their descendents claiming to be a nation apart from the parent stock.

—Gandhi

Bengal's Partition was announced in 1904 and annulled seven years later, in 1911. India's Partition was demanded in 1940 and executed seven years later, in 1947. If Congress had launched *Vande Mataram* movement to oppose Partition of Bengal in 1905, it announced Quit India movement to oppose India's Partition in 1943. The *Vande Mataram* movement was a grand success. It forced the British monarch to come down to India in order to declare partition null and void. But the Quit India movement, after having picked up a nationwide momentum, soon fizzled out. Gandhi himself admitted after a few months of its launch to Stewart Gelder, editor of the *News Chronicle* that the "Quit India movement had lapsed."

There are no 'if's and 'but's in history. But could the last seven years before partition be different? Could Jinnah be weakened? Could Partition be averted? Historians and authors take different views. The sequence of events too demonstrates that there were some moments during that momentous period that could have turned the tide against Jinnah and Partition. But what happened during those fateful years had a history of three decades behind it. Partition could have been averted, had the players been different. But they were those same Congress, League and British leaders who carried the mantle. It was two versus one in the end, with the British, atleast till Linlithgow was there as the Viceroy, firmly siding with Jinnah and abhorring Gandhi.

Long before Jinnah announced his support to the British openly, they had found in him an attractive option to work with. In November 1917, Edwin Montagu, Secretary of State for India, met with Jinnah during a visit to Bombay. He was so impressed by Jinnah's demeanor to declare that "it is, of course, an outrage that such a man should have no chance of running the affairs of his own country"[1].

Naturally, the British were impressed by Jinnah's Pakistan demand. British Prime Minister Winston Churchill used it to browbeat Congress. Churchill hated India and its religion. Hindus were "a beastly people with a beastly religion"[2] in his view. Churchill admired the book by an American author Beverley Nichols, Verdict on India, which was a toxic rant against Hindus and Congress. "I agree with the book and its conclusion – Pakistan", Churchill wrote to his wife[3]. He asked Viceroy Linlithgow to declare that the British "could not contemplate handing over power to any government the authority of which was directly denied by large and powerful elements in India's national life"[4]. By "large and powerful elements", Churchill meant Muslim League. Jinnah now had a veto, and the Congress leadership was naturally enraged.

Jinnah's agenda suited the British for another reason. The Second World War was on and Muslims constituted a large chunk of the British Indian Army which was actively involved in various theatres of war in Europe. The British needed the goodwill of Indian Muslims. It would have an impact on the Muslim allies of the British in the Middle East too. Linlithgow gleefully told London that Jinnah was a minority and he could hold his own with their support only.

Jinnah's relationship with Churchill continued after the latter lost the elections and became the leader of opposition in the British Parliament. Churchill suggested that the two leaders should not meet publicly. A covert channel was established between the two. Churchill would sign his secret missives as "GILLIATT". Together, they decided to scuttle any plan of the Labor Government to quit India before partitioning it. In a speech in the British Parliament in December 1946, Churchill denounced Atlee's plan to hand over power in India to the Congress. "In handing over the Government of India to these so-called political classes, we are handing over to men of straw of whom in a few years no trace will remain", he thundered[5].

Jinnah and the Muslim League prepared ground for this final parting of ways in the years before the Lahore conference. They found several excuses during the 1937-39 period when the Congress governments were in power in six out of eight provinces to propagate that justice won't be delivered to Muslims under the Hindu rule of the Congress. Everything that the governments did, significant or silly, like hoisting the tricolour or singing the truncated *Vande Mataram* or asking children in schools to say 'Namaste' – the typical Indian greeting was interpreted as an 'attack on Muslim culture'. Slowly but strategically they shifted the goalpost from separate electorates for Muslims to separate country for Muslims.

During the time that the League and Jinnah were upping the ante and trying to mobilise the entire Muslim opinion in their favour, the nationalists were in utter disarray and disunity. Congress was fighting with the League on one hand but also fighting with itself and other Hindu groups like the Hindu Mahasabha on the other.

Divisions within Congress became too stark at the time of election of Subhas Chandra Bose to the presidentship of the Congress. He became the Congress president in 1938. When he came forward for re-election in 1939, at the Tripuri session of the Congress in Madhya Pradesh, a dominant section of the Congress oldguard rose to oppose his candidature. Pattabhi Sitaramayya was put up against Bose, ostensibly with Gandhi's blessings. Sitaramayya was defeated by Bose even though he was physically not present due to ill-health.

These internal wranglings went on for months with the entire Congress organization coming to a standstill. Bose continued to remain in bed with illness. He was not allowed to form the Working Committee as the seniors like Gobind Ballabh Pant left sufficient hints insisting that the names that Bose would suggest for the Committee would be blocked by the AICC. Gandhi, although did not openly side with the dissidents, refused to intervene in the squabbles despite repeated requests by Bose. This was unusual of Gandhi, since in every other matter, whether the ego clashes between Nehru and Patel or Patel and Azad, he was always there as a mediator. Intense pressure continued to mount subsequently on Bose, forcing him to leave the Congress and start his own outfit called the Forward Bloc.

Bose was a force in Congress and the country. This parting of ways had hurt not only Congress but the unity of the nationalist forces at a time when the other side was making feverish efforts to unite all the Muslim parties and outfits under the fictitious narrative of "Islam in danger". First fallout of Bose's resignation was felt in the elections to the Calcutta Municipal Corporation. Although no longer the capital of India, Calcutta remained the largest and most diverse corporation in the country with Hindus, Muslims, the British and other Europeans having considerable voting populations. Bose took the unprecedented step of joining hands with the Muslim League at the elections to the chagrin of the Congress and the Hindu Mahasabha.

In the elections held in 1940, communal electorate system was implemented. Although Hindus constituted 70 per cent of the city's population, they were given only 47 seats in the 85-member corporation. When elections were held in March 1940, the Hindu seats were divided almost evenly between the Bose group in Congress (21 seats) and the Hindu Mahasabha under Syama Prasad Mookerjee (16 seats). The League won eighteen seats, eleven went to the Europeans and two to the British. Although emerging as the largest group, Bose decided to not only join hands with the Muslim League but also granted the mayor's post to the League nominee.

Although Bose defended the decision as a step to keep the League away from the British and the Europeans who were trying to capture Calcutta Municipal Corporation, neither Congress nor other nationalist Muslims were convinced.[6]

While criticising Bose for joining hands with the League

in Calcutta, strangely the Congress did the same thing in Karachi to defeat a genuinely nationalist Muslim leader and the premier of Sindh legislature, Allah Baksh Sumroo in 1940. Allah Baksh was the founder of the All-India Azad Muslim Conference, a large group of nationalist Muslims, who were opposed to Partition and the politics of Jinnah. Sumroo became the premier of Sindh in 1938. But when Muslim League brought a no-confidence motion against him in 1940, the Congress members in Sindh legislature extended support to the League, thus ending Allah Baksh's government.

The Azad Muslim Conference had a strong following in many provinces that became Pakistan later. It took a vociferously anti-Partition stance and even organised a big rally in Delhi in 1940. "No power on earth can rob anyone of his faith and convictions, and no power on earth shall be permitted to rob Indian Muslims of their just rights as Indian citizens," Allah Baksh declared.[7] Allah Baksh remained a nationalist and anti-partitionist till the end, and paid the price with his life in 1943, when he was murdered by unidentified youths due to the League's violent propaganda against him.

The Congress had a problem with the nationalist Hindus too, like the Hindu Mahasabha and others. In a resolution at the annual session in 1938, it denounced Hindu Mahasabha as communalist. Later, at the Congress session in August 1942, where the Quit India resolution was passed, Gandhi openly distanced himself from leaders of the Hindu Mahasabha, saying, "Those Hindus, who, like Dr. Munje and Shri Savarkar, believe in the doctrine of the sword, may seek to keep the Mussalmans under Hindu domination. I do not represent that section".[8]

Sadly, even the nationalist Muslims too had bitterly complained during that period that they were largely ignored or side-lined by the Congress leadership. League leadership used to deride them as 'Congress Muslims' and within the Congress, they "did not receive the strong ideological and political backing from the Congress. They were merely used on occasions, given decorative positions in the Congress hierarchy and loudly proclaimed as selfless and devoted leaders. At the same time, their point of view was often disregarded with undeserved contempt… they were treated at best as bargaining counters; when not so, they could easily be stored in the deep freeze".[9]

In his book, *India Wins Freedom*, Maulana Azad blames Gandhi for giving undue importance to Jinnah, and by implication, reducing the importance of so-called nationalist Muslims like him. "Jinnah had lost much of his political importance after he left the Congress in 1920s. It was largely due to Gandhiji's acts of commission and omission that Jinnah regained his importance in Indian political life," he writes grudgingly.[10] In an article in *Milli Gazette*. Dr. Mohammad Afsar Ali refers to a letter written by a 'patriotic Muslim leader' Habeebur Rehman to Gandhi, in which he says, "Yesterday, I read your statement. You are again ready to give Pakistan to Jinnah. The fact is that since Jinnah is a Gujarati, you love him and cannot forget him. You want to see him victorious despite his being wrong. This kind of gentle behaviour has strengthened the reactionary forces. Since Muslim League has passed the Pakistan resolution, you have been saying that if Muslims want it, they could be given Pakistan".[11]

It is too much of an exaggeration of Gandhi's views. Gandhi never said that Pakistan could be given if Muslims wanted it; what he said was that he was confident that majority of Muslims in India did not support Jinnah, but as a supporter of truth who would he be to say no if all of them wanted Partition and Pakistan! It was Gandhi's innate goodness and gentleness that had led to many such simplistic utterances by him which were prone to misinterpretations and misunderstanding. However, the fact remains that, like nationalist Hindus, nationalist Muslims too were unhappy with the Congress leadership at that time.

The third important nationalist and anti-partitionist force at that time was Hindu Mahasabha. Strangely, despite strong reservations about Muslim League's communal and divisive politics, Mahasabha saw it as 'pragmatic politics' to join hands with the League in provinces where it was in power. When the premier of Bengal, Fazlul Haq parted ways with Jinnah in 1941 over the latter's insistence that he quits the Imperial War Council, Hindu Mahasabha decided to support Haq. It joined Haq's ministry in Bengal in 1941 despite the fact that Haq was the prime mover of the Pakistan resolution at Lahore just a year ago. After the murder of Allah Baksh Sumroo, when a Muslim League government took power in Sindh provincial assembly, it was supported by the Hindu Mahasabha too. When League-led Sindh assembly passed a resolution demanding Pakistan in 1943, the Mahasabha members either walked out or did not vote, but they continued as ministers in the government. Same thing happened in the Frontier after the resignation of Khan Abdul Jabbar Khan as the premier in 1939 on the call of the Congress. In the League ministry of Sardar Aurangzeb Khan, there were Mahasabha members too. Aurangzeb Khan was one of the main organisers of the Lahore conference of the League a few months later.

In essence, on the nationalists' side, when the time came to stand up to League's partitionist politics, there was nobody. All were hobnobbing with all in the name of 'pragmatic politics' or because 'it was inevitable'.

On the other side, the overwhelming response that the League's call to the 'Day of Deliverance' received after the resignation of Congress ministries in six provinces, had boosted its morale and started attracting more and more prominent Muslim leaders, who were until then not supportive of Jinnah,.

With Viceroy Linlithgow openly supporting the League's claim as the sole representative of the Muslims of India, the scale certainly tilted in League's favour by the time the historic Lahore conference happened.

* * *

The Lahore Conference of the Muslim League, on March 22-24, 1940, was a big affair. The venue was Iqbal Park near Lahore Fort. Minar-e-Pakistan, a 60-m tall monument in the shape of a minaret stands there today as a historic monument of the Lahore Declaration. It was estimated that over one lakh people attended the inaugural session of the conference on the evening of March 22.

A couple of weeks before the conference, on March 9, Jinnah authored an article in *Time & Tide*, a magazine published from London, in which he repeated the unabashed and untruthful claim that Muslims were being subjected to atrocities in India under the Congress rule and the recognition of the Two-Nation Theory was the only solution. "An India-wide attack on the Muslims was launched. In the five Muslim provinces, every attempt was made to defeat the Muslim-led-coalition ministries...In the six Hindu provinces, a *kulturkampf* was inaugurated. Attempts were made to have 'Bande Mataram', the Congress Party song, recognised as the national anthem, the party flag and the real national language, Urdu, supplanted by Hindi. Everywhere oppression commenced and complaints poured in such force that the Muslims, despairing of the Viceroy and Governors ever taking action to protect them, have already been forced to ask for a Royal Commission to investigate their grievances," he blabbered.[12]

"Is it the desire (of British people) that India should become a totalitarian Hindu State....? ..... and I feel certain that Muslim India will never submit to such a position and will be forced to resist it with every means in their power," he further vehemently declared.[13]

Insisting that democracy was a guise under which a 'majority community rule' was being forced, he concluded that "a constitution must be evolved that recognizes that there are in India two nations, who both must share the governance of their common motherland."[14]

The Two-Nation Theory was first propagated by Mohammad Iqbal. At the Muslim League conference at Delhi in 1929, Iqbal proposed that Muslims of India should get a separate State. "I would like to see the Punjab, North-West Frontier Province, Sindh and Baluchistan amalgamated into a single State. Self-government within the British Empire, or without the British Empire, the formation of a consolidated north-west Indian Muslim State appears to me to be the final destiny of the Muslims, at least of north-west India," he said.[15]

After Iqbal's 'single state for Muslims' idea, a lesser-known student of Cambridge in London, Chaudhary Rahmat

Ali, a youngman in mid-thirties, came up with a pamphlet in January 1933 entitled "Now or Never – Are We to Live or Perish". In that, Rahmat Ali proposed a separate homeland for Muslims that included Punjab, Afghania (by which he meant NWFP), Kashmir, Sindh and Baluchistan. Although the pamphlet didn't explicitly call it Pakistan, later admirers of Rahmat attributed it to him as an acronym – P for Punjab, A for Afghania or NWFP, K for Kashmir, S for Sindh and Stan for Baluchistan. Once his pamphlet brought him fame and notoriety, Rahmat went ahead with more crazier geo-Islamist ideas like a greater Pakasia based on the ideology of Pak-ism.

Rahmat Ali also proposed in 1942 that India was never a nation, but a conglomerate of many religious groups. He used the word 'Dinia' (land of faith) for India and divided it up into twenty pieces. All Muslim enclaves were given a separate geographical identity. Bengal became 'Bangistan', Delhi 'Haidaristan', Hyderabad 'Osmanistan' and Malabar 'Maplistan'. If Europe could have 31 little countries, why not India, he argued.

It was around that time that the Communist leaders like Gangadhar Adhikari would forward the same ideology that India was never a nation but a conglomerate of nations.

Rahmat Ali and Jinnah met in 1934. But there was no record to show that Jinnah had endorsed the Pakistan idea in that meeting. Jinnah was still averse to communalization of his politics. But after his returned to India in 1936, a correspondence ensued between him and Iqbal in which Iqbal repeatedly exhorted Jinnah to demand for a separate Muslim State in north-west India "where they could spend their lives according to the teachings of the Holy Quran and

Sunnah of the Prophet (SAW)." The seeds of Pakistan were thus sown by Iqbal himself. Rahmat Ali provided a geography to it.

Although hesitant during the time when Iqbal was alive, Jinnah turned to the argument and got the Sindh provincial Muslim League to pass a resolution on those lines in October 1938. "In the interest of abiding peace of the vast Indian continent, and in the interest of unhampered cultural development, the economic and social betterment and political self-determination of the two nations, known as Hindus and Muslims, that India may be divided into two federations, viz. Federation of Muslim States and Federation of Non-Muslim States," the resolution read.[16]

The overwhelming support that the Lahore Conference got from Muslim masses was an indication of the growing clout of Jinnah, who by then had become universally recognised as *Quaid-e-Azam* – 'great leader' – by Muslims. Even leaders like Gandhi started calling him with that title in later years, although Jinnah, for the record, except once in 1944, consistently refused to address Gandhi as 'Mahatma'.

After the welcome address by Shah Nawaz Khan of Mamdot as the chairman of the local host committee, Jinnah rose to deliver the presidential address. His more than two-hour long English address was full of hyperbole and oversimplifications. He went on to call Hindus and Muslims as not just two different religious communities but two distinct civilisations and spoke about their different views on many issues.

"Hindus and the Muslims belong to two different religious philosophies, social customs and literature. They neither inter-marry nor inter-dine together, and, indeed, they belong to two different civilisations that are based mainly on conflicting ideas and conceptions. Their concepts on life and of life are different. It is quite clear that Hindus and Muslims derive their inspiration from different sources of history. They have different epics, different heroes and different episodes. Very often the hero of one is a foe of the other, and likewise, their victories and defeats overlap. To yoke together two such nations under a single State, one as a numerical minority and the other as a majority, must lead to growing discontent and final destruction of any fabric that may be so built up for the government of such a State", he said, claiming further that, "Mussalmans are a nation according to any definition of a nationhood. We wish our people to develop to the fullest spiritual, cultural, economic, social and political life in a way that we think best and in consonance with our own ideals and according to the genius of our people."[17]

During his speech, Jinnah quoted the letter written by Lala Lajpat Rai in 1924 to C.R. Das, in which he mentioned that Hindus and Muslims were two separate and distinct nations that could never be merged into a single nation. When Malik Barkat Ali claimed that Lala Lajpat Rai was a "nationalist Hindu leader", Jinnah responded, "No Hindu can be a nationalist. Every Hindu is a Hindu first and last."[18]

Jinnah's address made it clear that he was not going to settle for anything short of vivisection of India. He continued to peddle the Two-Nation Theory everywhere. "We are different beings. There is nothing in life which links us together. Our names, our cloths, our foods – they are all different; our economic life, our educational ideas, our treatment of women, our attitude to animals.. We challenge each other at every point of compass", he told a British journalist in 1944. Yet, interestingly, although he talked about Hindus and Muslims as two different nations, he did not explicitly use the word 'Pakistan' in his address.

The actual resolution, which later came to be recognised as the 'Pakistan Resolution', came up before the conference next day on March 23. It was moved by Fazlul Haq, the premier of Bengal and was seconded by Chaudhury Khaliquzzaman from the United Provinces, Zafar Ali Khan from Punjab, Aurangzeb Khan from NWFP and Abdullah Haroon from Sindh.

"No constitutional plan would be workable or acceptable to the Muslims unless geographical contiguous units are demarcated into regions, which should be so constituted with such territorial readjustments as may be necessary, that the areas in which the Muslims are numerically in majority as in the north-western and eastern zones of India should be grouped to constitute independent States in which the constituent units shall be autonomous and sovereign," the five-para resolution, clumsily drafted, insisted.[19]

"That adequate, effective and mandatory safeguards shall be specifically provided in the constitution for minorities in the units and in the regions for the protection of their religious, cultural, economic, political, administrative and other rights of the minorities, with their consultation. Arrangements thus should be made for the security of Muslims where they were in a minority," it also added.[20]

The resolution was finally adopted on the last day of the conference on March 24, although the Pakistanis erroneously decided to celebrate March 23 as the 'Pakistan Day'. Also, the resolution too did not use the word 'Pakistan' in it. Moreover, it talked about 'independent States' instead of one independent State for the Muslims. That had led to some confusion about the intent, with some arguing that the resolution was about creating two autonomous States on the north-west and the east of India. Muslim League took the initiative to clarify this point at the 28th annual conference of the League at Madras in 1941, where a resolution was adopted stating that "everyone should clearly understand that we are striving for one independent and sovereign Muslim State."[21] In his speeches, Jinnah too used to categorically talk about 'an independent homeland' or 'an independent Muslim State'.

With the passing of the Lahore Resolution, the Muslim demand in India conclusively shifted from 'separate electorates' to 'separate nation.'

Reference—

1. *Wolpert, Stanley (1984) "Jinnah of Pakistan" pp. 38, Oxford University Press*
2. *Louis, William Roger (1998), "Churchill and the Liquidation of the British Empire"America's National Churchill Museum accessed at https://www.nationalchurchillmuseum.org/kemper-lecture-roger.html*
3. *Bose, Mihir (2017), "From Midnight to Glorious Morning?" Haus Publishing*
4. *Menon, V.P. (1957), "The Transfer of Power in India" pp. 93, Sangam Books Ltd.*
5. *Mosley, Leonard (1965), "The Last Days of the British Raj" pp. 53, Jaico Books*
6. *Chatterjee, Pranab Kumar, "Proceedings of the Indian History Congress: Vol-41" p. 550-551*
7. *Ali, Dr. M.D. Afsar (2017), "Partition of India and Patriotism of Indian Muslims" accessed at https://www.milligazette.com/news/15756-partition-of-india-and-patriotism-of-indian-muslims/*
8. *"Gandhiji's Address before the AICC at Bombay on August 8, 1942" accessed at https://www.gandhiashramsevagram.org/gandhi-literature/quit-india-speeches-1942.php*

9. *Hassan, Mushirul (1995) "Builders of Modern India: M.A. Ansari" p. 161, Publications Division, Ministry of Information and Broadcasting, Government of India*
10. *Azad, Maulana Abul Kalam (1958), "India Wins Freedom" p. 81*
11. *Ali, Dr. M.D. Afsar (2017), "Partition of India and Patriotism of Indian Muslims" accessed at https://www.milligazette.com/news/15756-partition-of-india-and-patriotism-of-indian-muslims/*
12. *Jinnah, Mohammed Ali (1940), "The Constitutional Future of India: Two Nations in India" pp. 238-240, Time and Tide Vol.-21 p. 10*
13. *Ibid.*
14. *Ibid.*
15. *Jaffrelot, Christophe (2015), "The Pakistan Paradox: Instability and Resilience" p. 159, Oxford University Press*
16. *Ali, Dr. M.D. Afsar (2017), "Partition of India and Patriotism of Indian Muslims" accessed at https://www.milligazette.com/news/15756-partition-of-india-and-patriotism-of-indian-muslims/*
17. *"Address by Quaid-i-Azam Mohammad Ali Jinnah at Lahore Session of Muslim League" p. 5-23, Directorate of Films and Publishing, Ministry of Information and Broadcasting, Government of Pakistan, March 1940*
18. *"Lahore Resolution" accessed at https://historypak.com/lahore-resolution-1940/*
19. *Ibid.*
20. *Ibid.*
21. *Ibid.*

□

Quit India – Split Nationalists

We do not want any flag except the League flag Crescent and Star. Islam is our guide and a complete code of life. The Communists think we are fools. But they are mistaken... Hands off!

—M.A. Jinnah

The Muslim League's Lahore Resolution was full of irrational arguments. Yet, it demonstrated Jinnah's obduracy in forging ahead with his separatist agenda. It jolted the conscienceof the entire nation. It was the first official assertion of the Two-Nation Theory by Muslim League.

The Congress leaders were rattled. Jinnah's Pakistan was "mad and foolish and fantastic and... a huge barrier to all progress", Nehru fumed[1]. Gandhi realised that his efforts for Hindu-Muslim unity came to a naught and it was time for a more decisive action. From that realization was born the 'Quit India' Movement. On August 8, 1942, at the Mumbai session of the Congress, Gandhi launched the Quit India Movement with the unusually aggressive call of 'Do or Die'.

The Quit India Movement, also known as the August Revolution, was not only a belated response by Gandhi and the Congress to the threat posed by the Two-Nation

Theory of Jinnah and the Muslim League, but also a very hastily planned one. Gandhi, who stayed out of the Congress activities in the previous couple of years, ever since the Bose episode happened and internal squabbling increased, returned to the centre-stage during the Quit India Movement. He was greatly worried that the British were up to some serious mischief. Unless curtailed immediately, they would further exacerbate the Hindu-Muslim divide for their selfish imperial ends.

Gandhi was not entirely wrong. After the League resolution of 1940, Hindu-Muslim relations took a nosedive in the country. The British started aggressively pursuing their 'divide and rule' policy by promoting not only the League, but also whoever was seen opposing the Congress. Viceroy Linlithgow issued an open threat that if the Congress didn't support the British war efforts, in which some 2.3 million Indian soldiers were to be deployed to defend the Allied forces, the British Government would simply empower the Muslim League further. "The Hindu-Muslim feud was a bulwark of British India," Winston Churchill would confess years later.[2]

Jinnah had already declared an all-out war against Gandhi and the Congress, making wild allegations and widening the gulf between the communities. Gandhi realised that waiting for more time would only result in complete destruction of his dream project of freedom and unity.

Inside Congress, trusted Gandhi aide C. Rajagopalachari was taking a line that would help Jinnah. He brought a resolution in April 1942 at Madras suggesting that in order to secure a Congress – Muslim League entente, the Muslim provinces should be allowed to secede as a positive gesture from the Congress' side. In an attempt to please the power-seekers in Congress, he also brought another resolution that Congress should return to office in various provinces. Both resolutions were rejected. But they convinced Gandhi further about the urgent need for action.

When the Congress Working Committee met in July 1942, Gandhi placed his proposal before it for lunching a nation-wide agitation with the slogan of 'Quit India'. The Congress leadership was divided. Jawaharlal Nehru was by then actively campaigning in the country against Hitler's fascism. Suddenly, Gandhi asked him and others to oppose not only Hitler but the British too. It was a bitter pill for many. But Gandhi was adamant. Angered Rajagopalachari resigned from the Congress, protesting against the Quit India decision. He feared that Quit India would throw water on his proposal. Other senior leaders too were not very enthused, but they didn't have the courage to stop Gandhi. The proposal was accepted.

Meanwhile, this move got leaked to the media by the British agents, probably inside the Congress. That compelled the leadership to go in for it quickly. The Congress session was called at Bombay on August 8-10, 1942, in a hurry. It provided an opportunity to Gandhi to stir up the national sentiment with the slogan of 'Quit India'. On August 8, Gandhi addressed the enthusiastic crowds gathered at the Gowalia Tank Maidan in Bombay. Before he began his historic address, he got the Quit India Resolution presented by Jawaharlal Nehru. Nehru's call to the British to quit India was followed up by Sardar Patel, who said that the British should immediately hand over power to anyone –"thieves, robbers, and Muslim League – but you get out".

From the presidential chair, Azad put the Quit India Resolution to vote. It was carried with near unanimous support by the audience, who chanted "*Mahatma Gandhi ki Jai*."

After the passing of the resolution with overwhelming support, Gandhi rose to speak. Although he began by criticising the British for their intransigent attitude towards the question of India's Independence, he devoted a large part of the speech to Hindu-Muslim question. He did not hide the fact that he was influenced by the behaviour of the Muslim immigrants in South Africa, who had rallied behind him fully alongwith their Hindu counterparts, and "shed tears of grief at the separation" when he left for India in 1915. He had hoped that he would be able to repeat the same thing in India. With that hope, he extended full support to the Khilafat cause; even compromised on matters dear to his heart like cow protection in the spirit of not turning Khilafat into a bargain, Gandhi reminisced. "How then is that I have now come to be regarded as so evil and detestable?" he bemoaned.[3]

He reiterated his principled opposition to the Partition proposal, describing it as a "call to war". "To demand the vivisection of a living organism is to ask for its very life. It is a call to war. The Congress cannot be a party to such a fratricidal war," he insisted.[4]

If Pakistan was to remain a part of India, he wouldn't object to it, Gandhi suggested, adding that the Muslims must first join Hindus for securing freedom in that case. Describing Hindu-Muslim unity as a "matter of life and death" for him, he reiterated his oft-repeated line, "Millions of Mussalmans of this country came from Hindu stock. How can their homeland be any other than India? I ask the Mussalmans: 'If India is not your homeland, which other country do you belong to?' India is without doubt the homeland of all the Mussalmans inhabiting this country."[5]

Gandhi then came to the crux of the Quit India resolution. A leader, who once declared that he was willing to postpone the freedom struggle in order to achieve Hindu-Muslim unity, would now say that the freedom could not wait for anything anymore. "Freedom immediately, this very night, before dawn, if it can be had. Freedom cannot wait for the realisation of communal unity," he declared.[6]

Then came those famous words of his address: "Do or Die". "Here is a *mantra*, a short one, that I give to you. You may imprint it on your hearts and let every breath of yours give expression to it. The *mantra* is 'Do or Die'. We shall either free India or die in the attempt; we shall not live to see the perpetuation of our slavery. Every true Congressman or woman will join the struggle with inflexible determination not to remain alive to see the country in bondage and slavery."[7]

Gandhi's call for 'Do or Die' was radical for a man wedded to non-violence not just in action but in speech too. But Gandhi was careful and reminded Congressmen that the movement for civil disobedience as part of the Quit India campaign must be peaceful and non-violent. Gandhi was hoping to formally launch the movement on August 9 from the Congress session. However, on the night of August 8, the government swooped down on the Congress leadership and arrested almost all of them. A young Congress activist, Aruna Asaf Ali hoisted the Congress flag on August 9 to launch the agitation.

However, the actions of the British Government had resulted in the movement turning violent in many places. The leaderless agitation turned aggressive, initially giving jitters to the British. Viceroy Linlithgow described it as "by far the most serious rebellion since that of 1857."[8]

But the intensity didn't last long. The British clamped down on the agitators and arrested more than 100,000 of them. Press freedom was curbed. Senior leaders continued to languish in jails. More importantly, except for the Congress, all other nationalist groups stayed away from the movement. Rajagopalachari continued his efforts and tried to start a dialogue with not only the British but also the Muslim League by visiting the Congress leaders in jails.

Jinnah was initially perturbed by the intensity of the Quit India movement and called it the "most dangerous mass movement". He issued directions to all League units in the country to ensure that Muslims didn't participate in the programmes. To the Congress' call of 'Quit India', his retort was an appeal to the British to "divide and quit".

By early 1944, the 'Quit India' movement had petered out and effectively ended. That weakly planned movement had not achieved the dramatic results that Gandhi promised. Only positive response that came from the British side was the replacement of Lord Linlithgow with Lord Wavell, a more seasoned and balanced leader, as the Viceroy.

* * *

In the final analysis, the 'Quit India' movement can be termed as a failure. The British continued to rule to the utter disappointment of many Indians. During the movement, 'Quit India' slogans were scrawled and painted all across the country. After the movement's failure, there appeared "We wish we could" written underneath them displaying a sense of wry humour. Who should be blamed for this failure?

Gandhi's name comes to the mind first. As mentioned earlier, although he relinquished the primary membership of the Congress in 1934, Gandhi continued to attend all the important sessions of the Congress until the Quit India Movement. It was only after Gandhi's unilateral decision to re-engage with Jinnah in talks, in 1944, that the Congress leadership, including Nehru and Patel, started avoiding Gandhi in major decisions. He was there in the Bombay Congress session in 1942 when the 'Quit India' resolution was adopted, and he delivered that famous 'Do or Die' address there. Hence, he cannot fully absolve himself of the responsibility for its failure.

But then, he was not involved in the major decisions of the Congress and that included acceptance of the Partition plan. He used to learn about some of these only from the media. Technically speaking, the blame for later events could be put on the other leaders of the Congress. But Gandhi would always acquiesce to all those decisions of the leaders because he could not go against those whom he had himself nurtured and promoted.

Gandhi personified an interesting dichotomy. He could not get along with nationalist leaders and parties, like Savarkar and his Hindu Mahasabha or Subhash Bose and his Forward Bloc. Although he never shut his doors on them, he used important Congress forums to convey his differences with them. He used the Bombay session, where the 'Quit India' resolution was passed, to criticize the Hindu Mahasabha leadership. He remained a mute witness when Subhas was hounded out of the Congress after his victory against the official candidate at the Tripuri Congress session in 1939.

It can be called Gandhi's naivete or idealism, but he was a romantic democrat. He kept his engagement with all, irrespective of whether they supported him or otherwise. Savarkar, Ambedkar, Jinnah, Subhas Chandra Bose – all of them had differences with Gandhi on ideological grounds. Some of those differences were very profound and unbridgeable. Gandhi never compromised on his convictions and never hesitated to hide them to please anyone, but he never allowed those to come in the way of his engagement with all those leaders. He went to Ratnagiri to meet Savarkar in 1934. Savarkar categorically told him that the path Gandhi was treading would lead the country to doom. Gandhi disagreed and conveyed his disagreement with Savarkar at the Congress session in 1942.

Subhas Chandra Bose was also opposed to Gandhi ideologically as he believed that Gandhi's non-violence was not militant enough for achieving the Congress' objective of freedom. Infact, in May 1933, when he was in a sanitorium at Vienna, he happened to meet Vithalbhai Patel, the immediate elder brother of Sardar Vallabhbhai Patel. The two developed a good bond and issued the *Patel-Bose Manifesto*, which described Gandhi as a 'failed leader'. "Time has therefore come for a radical reorganisation of the Congress on a new principle and new method – non-co-operation will have to be changed into a more militant one."[9]

Subhas continued his opposition to Gandhi's non-violence programme. Yet, it was Gandhi who had made Bose the president of the Congress in 1938 despite serious opposition from no less a person than Sardar Patel. Sardar's antipathy for Bose had a personal dimension. He was involved in a peculiar feud with Bose in a family matter. Sardar's elder brother, Vithalbhai Patel, passed away at a young age, in Vienna. He was an admirer of Subhas. He had no children. It came to light after his death that Vithalbhai had executed a will bequeathing three-fourths of his money to "Mr. Subhas Chandra Bose (son of Janaki Bose) of 1 Woodburn Park, Calcutta" with the condition that the proceeds be used for "political uplift of India and preferably for publicity work on behalf of India's causes in other countries."[10] Clearly the will had intended the money to be used for revolutionary activities, which, in those days used to take place from foreign soil.

Sardar Patel had legally challenged this will in the courts. The case went on for years. Meanwhile, Bose became the Congress president in 1938 with Gandhi's blessings. Sardar was bitterly annoyed. He used all his energy next year to defeat Bose, but that too didn't succeed. Meanwhile, Patel had won the case in the Bombay High Court, but the bitterness remained. Bose fell out with Congress leadership and resigned from the Congress after his re-election in 1939. He launched the Forward Bloc first and raised the Azad Hind Fauj (Indian National Army, INA) afterwards to fight for India's freedom through military means.

With Ambedkar too, Gandhi's relations were not very cordial. Although Gandhi's determined opposition to separate electorates for the depressed classes through actions like 'fast unto death' had succeeded in persuading Ambedkar for the Poona Pact, Ambedkar was not too happy. But Gandhi never nursed any grudge against him. It was Gandhi's suggestion that had led to Ambedkar becoming the Law Minister in the first-ever cabinet of Jawaharlal Nehru in 1946. Later he became the chairman of the drafting committee of the Indian Constitution too.

But, on the other side, he consistently engaged with forces that were inimical to country's interests. Jinnah's and Muslim League's case is well-known, but less discussed is the case of the Communists. No discussion on Quit India Movement can conclude without discussing the treacherous role played by the Indian communists. It must be called treacherous because, unlike Hindu Mahasabha and Forward Bloc, which were treated by the Congress as enemies and never involved in the struggle, the Indian Communists were an integral part of the Congress movement for more than two decades. Their infiltration into the Indian freedom movement began well before the Communist Party of India was established in 1925.

Broadly, some of their aims, like the aims of many other groups, were in alignment with the aims of the mainstream Congress leadership, like Gandhi and Nehru. All were fighting against the British using different terminology. For the Communists, it was a fight against the capitalists and imperialists. But where they had major differences was with the method adopted by the Congress under Gandhi's direction. The Communists never supported non-violence. They backed the revolutionaries and their violent means for achieving freedom.

To his credit, Gandhi showed enormous tolerance towards the Communists, just as he was infinitely tolerant about Jinnah. When someone, irritated at Gandhi's persistent engagement with Jinnah, asked as to how he could continue with Jinnah's obduracy, Gandhi's reply was that God had given him enormous patience.

With Communism, Gandhi showed romantic idealism. He did not reject its philosophy, but he abhorred its methods. "I call myself a Communist also;"[11] "Classless society is the ideal, not merely to be aimed at but to be worked for;"[12] "What does Communism mean in the last analysis? It means a classless society – an ideal that is worth striving for,"[13] – he expressed such opinions in *Harijan* on different occasions. But he also wrote critically of Communism saying that "Communism of the Russian type, that is Communism which is imposed on a people, would be repugnant to India,"[14] and "Socialism and Communism of the West are based on certain conceptions, which are fundamentally different from ours. I do not subscribe to it."[15]

It was this romantic idealism that had led him to allow the Communists to have an important say in the affairs of the Congress all through the 1920s and 30s. Although the Socialist and Communist leaders like M.N. Roy, S.A. Dange, British Communist Leader Rajni Palme Dutt and others were openly critical, and occasionally abusive, of Gandhi and his policy of non-violence, Gandhi always treated them with undue respect and care. The Communist view was always sought at the Congress Working Committee meetings while drafting resolutions.

The Communists and the Socialists were a permanent fixture in the Congress organisation throughout the Independence movement. The Communists were expelled only in 1946 after all their misdeeds during the Quit India Movement, including their open collaboration with the British and, finally, their campaign for Partition of India and support for Muslim League in open defiance of the Congress' and Gandhi's line, became irreconcilable for leaders like Nehru and Patel. The Socialists left the

Congress after Independence to pursue their own political course.

The Communist members in the Congress were initially allowed full freedom because of two reasons. Jawaharlal Nehru, after attending the decennial celebrations of the Bolshevik Revolution in 1927 at Moscow, returned as a sympathizer of the Communist ideology. Although he denounced Communism later in 1936, his romance and obsession with Socialism continued even after Independence. Gandhi had serious problems with their ideology of revolution and violence, which he occasionally highlighted in his writings, but he too entertained a soft corner for their so-called concern of the oppressed classes. The result was that the Communists were allowed an active role in the Congress organisation. It allowed them to take over important Congress organisations like the All-India Trade Union Congress (AITUC), which was originally a trade union body sponsored by the Congress during the freedom struggle. The Congress was forced to start a separate trade union body by the name of Indian National Trade Union Congress (INTUC) later. In fact, the Communist cadres were active in the Congress organisation and even controlled some district committees in provinces like Punjab, Bengal and Uttar Pradesh.

Like all other groups, Gandhi demonstrated a similar attitude of accommodation towards the Communist members in the Congress organisation too. When the Communist leaders were arrested by the British in the Meerut Conspiracy Case, Gandhi went to the prison to meet them. He did the same with the revolutionaries of Bengal in 1937. (Gandhi faces some criticism for not coming in support of Bhagat Singh when he was sent to the gallows in 1931.

Gandhi disagreed with methods that involved violence. Days before Bhagat Singh's execution by the British, Gandhi was with Viceroy Irwin negotiating on behalf of the Congress. Could he have forcefully raised Bhagat Singh's case with Irwin and got it commuted to a lesser one? Why did he not do that? These pertinent questions remain.) At the Ramgarh session of the Congress in 1940, a top underground Communist leader was escorted by Gandhi in his own car to the Subjects Committee meeting, in order for him to move the Communist amendments to the draft resolution.

The Communist leadership, although disagreeing with Gandhi's programme, broadly remained in line with the objective of Independence until then. But trouble started brewing with the advent of the Second World War in 1939. In the initial years of the war, Stalin was in a secret deal with Hitler and the Nazis as it suited the Communist agenda of denouncing the imperialist West. Hence it was touted as an anti-imperialist war by the Communists. Congress was divided. Nehru was unwilling to support the British unless they unequivocally committed to grand India freedom after the war. Gandhi and other were of the view that the British must be supported at a time when they were engaged in a just war against the dictatorial and fascist forces.

But that was not the Communist propaganda line at that time. They were following instructions from the Comintern leadership in London, which had advised them to brand the war as "anti-imperialist war" and oppose British war efforts in India. At the Ramgarh session of the Congress, the Communist leaders had raised slogans, like "*Yeh ladai samrajyashahi, na ek pai, na ek bhai*" (This is a war of the imperialists, not a pie for it to be given, nobody to join it).

However, in June 1941, Hitler turned his tanks towards Moscow after capturing Poland. As the armies of Hitler started marching towards Russia, intense debates erupted in India over the war. Towards the end of 1941, Japan too entered the war and captured Burma and Singapore from the British. Subhas Bose was forming his Azad Hind Fauj to fight the British for freedom at that time. He had the support of the Japanese Army.

In Congress, roles reversed. Nehru, the "sole foreign policy expert" in Congress, launched a nation-wide campaign against Hitler to the utter delight of the Communists and the British. On the other hand, Gandhi became the voice of the group calling for pressurizing the British to commit for independence while the war was on. Against the wishes of many in Congress, Gandhi managed to get the Quit India Movement launched in August 1942.

Communists in Congress were greatly upset over this development. Already, most Communist leaders were in prisons because the British Government had arrested them for their campaign against the Allied forces and calling the war 'imperialist'. A few of the Communist members that attended the Bombay session of the Congress in 1942 tried to oppose the 'Quit India' resolution unsuccessfully. By then, they had received a new Comintern communique from the British Communist Party leader Harry Pollitt that the war overnight should be rechristened as "people's war" since Stalin joined hands with the Allied forces and Hitler became the common enemy for both the Western imperialists and the Soviet communists. Although they could not stop Quit India resolution, the Communists received a pat on their back from none other than Gandhi, who complimented them in his speech for their courage to dissent, to "learn not to lose courage even when we are in a hopeless minority."[16]

Around the time when Gandhi launched his final battle for unity and independence of India, secretary of the Communist Party of India, Gangadhar Adhikari, came out with a horrendous thesis openly supporting the demand of the Muslim League for Pakistan. The so-called position paper with the title "Pakistan and National Unity" became famous as "Adhikari Thesis". It argued that India was never a united country "from Kashmir to Kanyakumari" and the idea of "one nation, one people, one language" never existed at any point in history. It then concluded that all the different regions of India were "different individual nationalities."[17]

"The Lingayat peasantry of Karnatak... wakes up to anti-imperialist consciousness and develops a natural yearning for a free Karnatak... So it is with the Andhra, Tamils and with the Sindhis, Punjabis and the Pathans... as soon as we grasp that behind the demand for Pakistan is the justified desire of the people of Muslim nationalities such as Sindhis, Baluchis, Punjabis (Muslims), Pathans to build their free national life... there is a very simple solution to the communal problem in its new phase... nationalities, such as Sindhis, Baluchis, Pathans and Punjabi Muslims have the right to secede if they so desire... wherever people of Muslim faith living together in a territorial unit, form a nationality... they certainly have the right to autonomous state existence," Adhikari's paper argued.[18]

The Communist Party of India (CPI) had not only endorsed it but passed a resolution to the effect based on this paper.

As the Quit India struggle was raging in the country, the Communists decided to sabotage it from within and without. They started communicating with the British with the offer of assistance during the war. It suited the British as they were struggling to cope with the Congress onslaught of Quit India. Many Communist leaders, prominent among them were B.T. Ranadive and P.C. Joshi, were released from detention and became open saboteurs helping the British officers and administration at many places in the country against the Congress. When the 'Quit India' campaigners tried to organise *hartals* and *bandhs,* the Communist cadres and their trade unions tried their best to fail those strikes and *hartals*. The Communist cadres became the informers for the British, passing on information on the whereabouts of the agitators, leading to the capture and arrest of many of the leaders of the Quit India Movement.

Communist Party's new tactical line and new propaganda now started to function. They attacked national organisations for their stand against the unity and security of India. They organised public speeches and attacked Subhas Chandra Bose calling him the "running dog of imperialists". The party was organising pro-British propaganda, like "National Unity Week" when others were fighting for freedom.

"The party even organised public programmes for Hindu-Muslim unity as part of its tactical line to support the British. And they were the first people to support division of India into Muslim Pakistan! CPI blamed all nationalist organisations and people as fifth columnists! It can be seen in all of their letters to British and we can find remarks by British in which CPI seems to be referring everyone else as fifth columnists! In fact, CPI was doing the real job of fifth columnists," states a well-researched paper.[19]

Arun Shourie, when he was the editor of *The Indian*

Express in mid-1980s, was once invited by a group of students at the Jawaharlal Nehru University (JNU) in Delhi for a late-night conversation on the campus, where he thoroughly exposed the duplicity of the Communists during the Quit India Movement. When a Left student tried to heckle him by asking how much he was paid by the CIA to run the campaign, the following exchange of words took place between them:

Arun Shourie (AS): Are you a student or a teacher?

Student: I am a student.

AS: For how long?

Student: 10 years.

AS: I asked this question because I wanted to ensure whether you are contaminated or the one doing the contaminating.[20]

Arun Shourie later penned a four-part series in the now-defunct *Illustrated Weekly of India* under the title "The Great Betrayal". It exposed in great detail the treacherous role played by the Communists during and after the Quit India Movement, including the correspondence between the Communist leaders and the British officials. He later authored a book on the theme titled "The Only fatherland".

Although the generation after Independence got to know about the acts of omission and commission by the Communists during the final years of the freedom struggle much later through the writings of Arun Shourie (*The Only Fatherland*) and Minoo Masani (*The Communist Party of India – A Short History*), the Congress leaders of that time had first-hand experience of their treachery. As a result, the Communists got isolated in the Congress and finally forced to leave in 1946. Some Communist leaders, like Mohan

Kumaramangalam, reached out to Gandhi with 'explanations', but that didn't cut much ice. Kumaramangalam later joined the Congress and became a minister in the Nehru's cabinet.

People's Democracy, the mouthpiece of the Communist Party, had disclosed many years later that the party had reviewed the stand during the Quit India Movement and concluded that "...the party committed serious mistakes for which it had to pay a heavy price. While correctly supporting the people's war, it failed to integrate the contradiction in the international sphere with the national-level contradiction. While the struggle against fascism was the main contradiction in the international sphere, at the national level, the contradiction between the people and British imperialism was dominant. It was therefore wrong on the part of the party to oppose the 'Quit India' movement and adopt a line of avoiding mass struggle on the plea that it would damage the war effort."[21]

Reference—

1. *Hajari, Nisid (2015), "Midnight's Furies: The Deadly Legacy of India's Partition" pp. 43, Houghton Mifflin Harcourt*
2. *Boissoneault, Lorraine (2017): The Speech That Brought India to the Brink of Independence'. Accessed at https://www.smithsonianmag.com/history/speech-brought-india-brink-independence-180964366/*
3. *Gandhi, Mahatma (1942): The 'Quit India' Speeches. Accessed at https://www.gandhiashramsevagram.org/gandhi-literature/quit-india-speeches-1942.php*
4. *Ibid*
5. *Tendulkar, D.G.: Mahatma, Vol.-VI, p. 197, Bombay K. Jhaveri and D.G Tendulkar*
6. *Gandhi, Mahatma (1942): The 'Quit India' Speeches. Accessed at https://www.gandhiashramsevagram.org/gandhi-literature/quit-india-speeches-1942.php*
7. *Ibid*

8. *Singh, Anita Inder (1987): The Origins of the Partition of India: 1936-1947, pp. 85, Oxford University Press, Delhi*
9. *Patel, Vithalbhai Jhaverbhai (1995): Selected Works of Vithalbhai J. Patel: 1933, p. 1518, Mittal Publications*
10. *Ghose, Sanjay (2020): When NetajiSubhas Fought a Case in the Bombay HC. Accessed at https://www.livelaw.in/columns/when-netaji-subhas-fought-a-case-in-the-bombay-hc-162806*
11. *Gandhi, M.K. (August 4, 1946), Harijan, Vol.-X, p. 26*
12. *Gandhi, M.K. (March 13, 1937), Harijan, Vol.-V, p. 5*
13. *Ibid*
14. *Gandhi, M.K. (February 13, 1937): Harijan, Vol.-V, p. 1*
15. *Gandhi, M.K. (August 2, 1934): Anand Bazar Patrika*
16. *Gandhi, Mahatma (1942): The 'Quit India' Speeches. Accessed at https://www.gandhiashramsevagram.org/gandhi-literature/quit-india-speeches-1942.php*
17. *Balakrishna, Sandeep (2016): The Unaccountable Communist Republic of JNU. Accessed at https://www.dailyo.in/politics/jnu-kanhaiya-kumar-anti-national-sedition-soviet-union-marxism-cpim-left-front-congress-indira-gandhi-9506*
18. *Ed. Adhikari, Gangadhar: Pakistan and National Unity, p. 4, People's Publishing House, Bombay*
19. *Communist Betrayal of Indian Independence Movement: 1942 Secret British Indian Files. Accessed at https://indictales.com/2019/09/02/communist-betrayal-of-indian-independence-movement-1942-secret-british-india-files/*
20. *Balakrishna, Sandeep: The Communist Death Vault: A Little Known Anecdote about JNU. Accessed at https://www.dharmadispatch.in/commentary/the-communist-death-vault-a-little-known-anecdote-about-jnu*
21. *People's War and Quit India Movement. Accessed at https://peoplesdemocracy.in/2020/0308_pd/people's-war-and-quit-india-movement*

□

Jinnah – With 'Pistol In Hand'

Gandhiji's approach to Mr. Jinnah on the occasion was a great political blunder. It gave a new and added importance to Mr. Jinnah which he later exploited to the full

—Abul Kalam Azad

Gandhi had launched the Quit India Movement as he realised that his earlier efforts at winning over the Muslims to his side were not working. He was flabbergasted at the rejection of his leadership by the Indian Muslims despite his sincere efforts, that included several compromises and acts of appeasement. He made his disappointment public in the speech at the 'Quit India' session of the Congress at Bombay.

He realised that it would be a big let down to those millions who trusted him if the country was divided on Hindu-Muslim lines. He understood that the situation was slipping out of his hands. Hence, "unity at all costs" became his mission after he was released from detention in 1944. But the next three years leading to Partition of India were to remain the saddest part of his life.

The year 1944 began on a sad note for Gandhi. His wife of six decades, Kasturba Gandhi, died in his lap on February

22, 1944 at the Aga Khan Palace in Poona where he was incarcerated by the British. Kasturba was by his side in his struggles – both personal and political – right from the Transvaal *satyagraha* days in South Africa. She continued to take part in every Congress movement for Independence, with or without Gandhi by her side. Gandhi was in prison when she fell seriously ill and was taken to the Aga Khan Palace as per her desire to be by his side in the last days of her life.

"She helped me to keep wide awake and true to my vows. She stood by me in all my political fights and never hesitated to take the plunge. In the current sense of the word, she was uneducated; but to my mind she was a model of true education," Gandhi wrote poignantly, paying tribute to Kasturba. "If anything, she stood above me. But for her unfailing co-operation I might have been in the abyss," he added.[1]

Gandhi loved Kasturba dearly and her death naturally caused immense pain to him. He refused to leave the funeral ground for a couple of hours until her body was completely consigned to flames.

Loneliness engulfed Gandhi after Kasturba's death. All senior leaders including Nehru and Patel were in jails. Others, like Rajaji, had parted ways. Moreover, Gandhi was not in the best of his health too. The twenty-one-day fast that he had undertaken in 1943, in which he narrowly escaped from the jaws of death, had its effect on the seventy-seven-year-old body. The new Viceroy Wavell had decided to set Gandhi free from prison. Gandhi first moved to Bombay and later to the hill station of Panchgani to recuperate.

Meanwhile, sometime in 1943, C. Rajagopalachari,

who had quit the Congress over the 'Quit India' resolution, approached Gandhi, when the latter was at the Yerawada Jail in Poona, with a formula for Congress-Muslim League thaw. Known as the C.R. Formula, it proposed that if the League endorsed the Congress demand for national Independence during the pendency of the war, Congress would agree to the demarcation of contiguous Muslim-majority districts in the north-west and north-east of India after the war. A plebiscite would then be conducted in those areas on the basis of adult franchise over the demand for Pakistan. In case the vote went in favour of constituting two separate States, there will be an agreement between the two over issues like defence, foreign affairs, commerce, communications and other areas of mutual concern.

When Gandhi showed interest in engaging with Jinnah on the basis of C.R. Formula, Rajagopalachari approached Jinnah with the same proposal. Jinnah immediately dismissed it, describing it as a "shadow and a husk, a maimed and moth-eaten Pakistan".[2] The formula was shelved.

But after the release of Gandhi from prison, Rajagopalachari approached him once again with the same proposal. Desperate to prevent the country's division at any cost, Gandhi was keen to establish contact with Jinnah once again. Rajagopalachari then reached out to Jinnah in August 1944, with his formula the second time. Jinnah didn't outrightly reject it this time. Instead, he promised to place it before the League's Working Committee. But Jinnah, the clever lawyer he was, immediately started projecting in C.R.'s formula Gandhi's indirect acceptance of the "principle of Partition or the division of India".

Gandhi had not; he was only keen on making a last-ditch attempt to compel Jinnah to see reason and give up the demand for a separate nation. He saw in the C.R. Formula an opportunity to reconnect with his active challenger. Although taken by Gandhi in good spirit, that decision would only help in further increasing the stature of Jinnah in the eyes of the Muslims as well as the British. Jinnah was in a way lucky. Two of his main challengers among the Muslims, Sir Sikandar Hayat Khan and Allah Baksh Sumroo died in quick succession. Hayat Khan, the premier of Punjab died in December 1942 while Sumroo was murdered by zealous Muslim League cadre in May 1943. And best thing was, the great Gandhi had come calling. He was now truly the "sole spokesman" of the Indian Muslims.

The Congress leadership, languishing in jail, was horrified at Gandhi's decision to open talks with Jinnah at this juncture. Nehru always held Jinnah in contempt. In December 1943, he recorded in his prison diary that the Muslim League leader represented "an obvious example of the utter lack of civilized mind"[3]. He was seriously put off by Jinnah's three-hour long address at the League meeting in Delhi. He described it as "blatant, vulgar, offensive, egoistical, vague... What a man! And what a misfortune for India and for the Muslims that he should have so much influence". He attributed Jinnah's popularity to "opportunism raised to the nth degree, pomposity and filthy language, abuse... a capacity for what is considered 'clever' politics, vulgarity... total incomprehension of the events & forces that are shaping the world"[4]. But he knew that nobody could stop Gandhi from what he intended to do once he made up his mind. Gandhi anyway had his weapon – that he was not even an ordinary member of the Congress, and hence his actions were not binding on anybody.

Despite Jinnah's mischief and procrastination, Gandhi persisted. "Let us meet whenever you wish. Do not disappoint me," he wrote to Jinnah.[5] The two finally met at Bombay. For full nineteen days, from September 9 to 27, 1944, Gandhi climbed up the steps of Jinnah's place, "almost daily, and sometimes even twice in a day." The two met for three hours on the first day; they met again after two days, and again next day, a day after... Talks went on and on. Finally, on September 27, Jinnah announced that the talks had failed. They were bound to. Jinnah had indicated that he wouldn't regard C.R. Formula worth considering as it put the "cart before the horse".[6] During his dialogue with Gandhi, Jinnah accused that the C.R. Formula had actually made the Lahore resolution not only 'out of shape' but 'mutilated it'.

While Gandhi saw the C.R. Formula as an opportunity to atleast keep India united despite agreeing for rearrangement of provinces on communal lines, Jinnah saw it as "calculated to completely torpedo the Pakistan demand of Muslim India."[7] Jinnah was categorical on several points: Congress should immediately withdraw the call for 'Quit India'; it should agree that Hindus and Muslims constituted two separate nations; their geographical regions shouldn't be tampered with in the name of plebiscite or whatever; no question of any common subjects as the two States would be totally independent and sovereign; finally, Congress should agree for Partition first, and then freedom.

A year of sorrow and disappointment for Gandhi would, however, end on a pleasant note. October 2, 1944 marked the seventy-fifth birthday of Gandhi. Greetings and good wishes poured in from all over the world. Albert Einstein, a world-renowned physicist sent a moving message, describing Gandhi as "a leader of his people, unsupported by any outward authority; a politician whose success rests not upon craft, nor upon mastery of the technical devices, but simply on the convincing power of his personality; a victorious fighter, who has always scorned the use of force; a man of wisdom and humility; armed with resolve and inflexible consistency; who has devoted all his strength to the uplifting of his people and the betterment of their lot; a man who has confronted the brutality of Europe with the dignity of the simple human being, and thus at all times superior". He ended his greetings with these famous words: "Generations to come, it may be, will scarce believe that such a one as this ever in flesh and blood, walked upon this earth."[8]

Subhas Chandra Bose, who had by then launched his war against the British with his Indian National Army (INA), sent wishes from Rangoon, seeking Gandhi's "blessings and good wishes in this holy war for India's liberation."[9] Bose had, for the first time, coined the phrase "Father of our Nation" in his birthday message.

There was one person though, who would not greet Gandhi on that day. That was Jinnah.

* * *

Things started deteriorating afterwards. As the war in Europe ended in favour of the Allied forces, the British once again turned their attention towards the Indian situation. They clearly saw the widening gulf between the Congress and the League and decided to play up the same. They also noticed that the failure of the Quit India Movement had dampened the spirits of Congress cadres in the country while the same had an opposite effect on Jinnah, who became more and more hostile.

Viceroy Wavell made the first move by announcing in

June 1945 that since Indian parties were unable to come to an understanding among themselves over the form of the self-governing institutions, the British would reconstitute the Executive Council by providing extended participation for different groups. This was a mischievous move by the British by which they wanted to reject Congress's main demand for Independence, while at the same time tried and exacerbated more divisions within Indian society.

As per Wavell's plan, there would be parity in representation. So, he gave five seats to 'caste Hindus' and five to the Muslims. A separate representation was announced for the Scheduled Castes although the Poona Pact explicitly rejected British attempts to divide Hindu society. This brazen act of the Viceroy agitated not only the Congress and Gandhi but also others, like Savarkar, Syama Prasad Mookerjee and Madan Mohan Malviya. Gandhi was livid and insisted that the expression "caste Hindus" be removed. He was also aghast at the parity between Hindus and Muslims although their populations were two-third and one-third, respectively.

But when the leaders of all parties met Wavell at Shimla in June 1945 to finalise the proposal, the Congress leadership was willing to join hands. Instead of arguing over questions like parity and 'caste Hindu' nomenclature, the Congress leadership, led by Azad, was insistent on nominating a Muslim from its side to the Council. That would have left Hindus in a minority in the nine-member EC.

By then, Jinnah, having tasted some success, became more obstinate and insisted that Congress had no right to nominate any Muslim. The Muslim representation in the EC should come only from the Muslim League, Jinnah insisted.

"All other minorities, such as Scheduled Castes, Sikhs and the Christians have the same goal as the Congress... Their goal and ideology is... of a united India. Ethnically and culturally, they are very closely knitted to Hindu society," Jinnah argued, demanding fifty percent representation for the Muslims in any constitutional body to be created.[10] Wavell's proposal had to be shelved due to Jinnah's intransigence.

In the elections held to the British Parliament in July 1945, power changed hands. Churchill and the Conservatives were defeated and Clement Atlee, leader of the Labour Party, became the Prime Minister. Atlee decided to hold elections to the Central and provincial legislatures in India. The elections were conducted in December that year. Franchise was limited to hardly ten percent of the population.

Jinnah, who faced a humiliating defeat in 1937 provincial elections, was careful this time. He unleashed a massive negative campaign on crass communal lines. The results demonstrated that his communal bigotry worked.

In the provincial elections, the Muslim League secured good victories in Muslim seats although it fell short of absolute majority in many provinces. Congress too secured good victories in the election. It won over 90% of the non-Muslim votes. Its governments came into power in six provinces – Bihar, UP, CP, Bombay, Madras, Orissa, Assam and NWFP. In NWFP, which became Khyber Pakhtunkhwa in 2010, Congress secured a huge majority. In Punjab, Congress and Akalis together secured equal number of seats as the League. The League swept Muslim seats in Hindu-majority provinces. It also won a majority in two provinces – Sindh and Bengal. Although this was a better performance for Jinnah compared to the 1937 elections, his pet 'Pakistan' thesis continued to hang in fire. Two important Muslim provinces – NWFP and Punjab still eluded him. Khan Brothers continued their domination in NWFP, while Punjab remained under the control of the Unionists. The 1946 elections were a tragic testimony to the fact that areas that had not voted for the Muslim League had become Pakistan later, while those Muslim areas that overwhelmingly supported the League remained in India.

By 1946, things deteriorated further for the British. As the trials of eleven INA officers progressed at the Red Fort in India, nationalist fervor started resurging in the country. There were revolts in the Royal Indian Navy and the unrest spread to some Army cantonments also. Viceroy Wavell and his Commander-in-Chief Auchinleck realized that it would be difficult to depend on the large Indian contingent in their military.

Atlee understood the situation and despatched a delegation led by Sir Pethick Lawrence, a senior Labour politician to finalise a plan for handing over power to the Indians. Known as the Cabinet Mission, the three-member delegation had Stafford Cripps of the Cripps Mission fame and A.V. Alexander as the other members. The Mission, which arrived in March 1946, announced the proposal that there would be a two-tier arrangement in governance of the country. There would be a Central government dealing with defence, external affairs and communications while the provinces would be grouped into two – Hindu and Muslim provinces – and all other matters would be handled by the groups.

A conference was called at Shimla in May to finalise the plan, but no agreement could be reached at. The Cabinet

Mission went ahead and announced a modified plan under which there would be a weak Central Government dealing with three subjects – defence, foreign affairs and communications – and the rest of the country would be divided into three groups of provinces, instead of two. Group A would be Hindu provinces, Group B would be the Muslim provinces of the northwest and Group C would be Muslim provinces of the northeast.

Jinnah was initially adamant on Pakistan and insisted that all five Muslim provinces should be clubbed together and handed over to the League. Pethick Lawrence warned him that he could not allow him to control the destiny of forty-three per cent population of India, which consisted of a large number of Hindus also. The option could have been to Partition Bengal and Punjab, for which the Cabinet Mission was not empowered. He advised Jinnah to accept the plan. Jinnah understood the situation and decided to seize the limited opportunity offered to him by the British. In June, the Muslim League Working Committee endorsed the Cabinet Mission plan.

Gandhi was skeptical about it. He could not digest the communal division of the provinces. He was also unsure about the possibility of a Central Government that would be so weak as to have no powers internally. He conveyed his reservations when the Congress Working Committee met in June. The Congress leadership, including Nehru, Patel and Azad, had by then made up their minds to accept the plan because it was the first ever offer by the British to transfer power into the hands of Indians. It would give Congress the leadership of the first Indian Government, however weak it might be .

Gandhi faced humiliation at the hands of his own

mentees for the first time. Gandhi was used to 'emotional bargain' in the past, whenever he faced a challenge inside the Congress. He tried the same this time too, telling the Working Committee that "I admit defeat. You should follow my intuition only if it appeals to your reason; otherwise, you should take an independent course. I shall now leave with your permission. You should follow the dictates of your reason."[11] On earlier occasions, when Gandhi said something like this, the leaders would have urged him to stay on, with the promise that they would follow his instinct.

But this did not happen that way. Pyarelal gives a graphic account: "A hush fell over the gathering. Nobody spoke for sometime. The Maulana Saheb with his unfailing alertness at once took in the situation. 'What do you desire? Is there any need to detain Bapu any further?' he asked. Everybody was silent. Everybody understood. In that hour of decision, they had no use for Bapu. They decided to drop the pilot. Bapu returned to his residence"[12].

When the Working Committee met again at noon, Gandhi was not even invited. Needless to say, the committee gave its assent to the plan. This discord continued until the country was partitioned while securing Independence. Gandhi would largely remain a bystander in all important decisions. He finally displayed his displeasure by refusing to stay in Delhi on August 15, 1947, when Independence was finally achieved, despite appeals from all senior leaders.

The ship finally anchored on the shores, much battered, *albeit* without its captain.

* * *

Gandhi was proven right. Differences cropped up between Congress and Muslim League at the very outset and that left the Cabinet Mission plan a non-starter.

On July 10, 1946, Jawaharlal called a rather aggressive seventy-five-minute press conference at the Congress House in Bombay, in which he claimed that the Congress agreed only to enter the Constituent Assembly to be constituted under the Cabinet Mission plan and nothing else. He in fact argued in front of the media that it was not to Congress' liking that we had a weak Centre.

"It is obvious that without the Central authority, you cannot deal with the problems mentioned above. There must be some overall power to intervene in a grave crisis, breakdown of the administration, or economic breakdown, or famine. The scope of the Centre, even though limited, inevitably grows because it cannot exist otherwise. Though some people oppose this broadening of the Centre, the Constituent Assembly will have to decide on the point," Nehru insisted.[13]

He ridiculed the Muslim League and insisted that except for the League, nobody else wanted the grouping of the provinces. "Everybody outside the Muslim League was entirely opposed to grouping. In regard to this matter, the Muslim League stands by itself isolated," he said. And then Nehru made the most explicit statement: "The big probability is that, from any approach to the question, there will be no grouping."[14]

Jinnah was livid. He saw in Nehru's statement a design to snub the League. He was in fact not happy with the plan right from the beginning. Nehru's statements gave him an opportunity to wriggle out. He accused that the Congress leadership was insincere. An urgent meeting of the League leadership was called, and it was decided that the League would withdraw from the Cabinet Mission Plan. In fact, Jinnah declared on a later occasion that the League would now abandon all constitutional means.

Nehru's outbursts came as a surprise to other Congress leaders. Many of them were angry and upset with Nehru. Maulana Azad, who had just handed over the presidency of the Congress to Nehru, said, "Now happened one of those unfortunate events which changed the course of history... He (Jawaharlal) is at times apt to be carried away by his feelings. Not only so, but sometimes he is so impressed by theoretical considerations that he is apt to underestimate the realities of a situation."[15]

Sardar Patel called it Nehru's 'emotional insanity'. He criticised Nehru for acting with "childlike innocence, which puts us all in difficulties quite unexpectedly... and puts tremendous strain on us to set matters right."[16]

There were efforts to salvage the situation. At the Congress Working Committee meeting in early August, Azad suggested that Congress issue a statement clarifying that Nehru's statement was his personal view. But Nehru was unhappy; he said that it would be an embarrassment not only to the Congress but personally for him. The effort was shelved.

In any case, by then, Jinnah had already announced his decision of walking back on the Cabinet Mission plan. He told the British that since it was the Congress leadership which had backtracked from the original agreement, he should be given the opportunity to lead the Constituent Assembly. When no response came from the British for his bizarre demand, Jinnah hurriedly called the League Council meeting in July end and announced his decision.

That was the end of the Cabinet Mission plan and the beginning of the most sordid phase of the Independence movement.

* * *

A week after Nehru's press conference, Jinnah made his anger public for the first time addressing his supporters on July 19. "League had lost faith in constitutions and constitutional methods," he declared. "Throughout the painful negotiations, the two parties with whom we bargained held a pistol at us: one with power and machine guns behind it, and the other with non-co-operation and the threat to launch mass civil disobedience. This situation must be met. We also have a pistol," he added belligerently.[17]

At the urgently called council meeting of the Muslim League on July 29, a resolution was adopted calling for organising August 16, 1946 as the Direct Action Day. "We do not want war. If you want war, we accept your offer unhesitatingly. We will either have a divided India or a destroyed India," Jinnah threatened the Congress.[18]

Jinnah's choice of the date was deliberate. August was the month of Ramzan and August 16 was a Friday. Naturally Muslims assembled in mosques in large numbers. The League members distributed handbills calling upon Muslims to "brave the rains and all difficulties and make the Direct Action Day meeting a historic mass mobilisation of the *millat*."[19]

This is from a pamphlet written by the Calcutta Mayor S.M. Usman: "...By the grace of God, we are crores in India but through bad luck we have become slaves of Hindus and the British. We are starting a *jihad* in your name in this very month of Ramzan... Give your helping hand in all our actions—make us victorious over the *kaffirs* – enable us to establish the kingdom of Islam in India... by the grace of God, may we build up in India the greatest Islamic kingdom in the world..."[20]

On August 13, 1946, the Muslim League's mouthpiece, *Star of India*, gave detailed instructions to the League cadres in particular and Muslims in general on how to conduct themselves on August 16 - the Direct Action Day. Muslims were in the middle of Ramzan fasting and the *Star of India* reminded them of "the month of real *jihad* of God's grace and blessings, and spiritual armament and moral and physical purge of the nation... Muslims must remember that it was in Ramzan that the Quran was revealed. It was in Ramzan that the permission for *jihad* was granted by Allah. It was in Ramzan that the battle of Badr, the first open conflict between Islam and Heathenism, was fought and won by 313 Muslims and again it was in Ramzan that 10,000 Muslims under the Holy Prophet conquered Mecca and established the kingdom of Heaven and the Commonwealth of Islam in Arabia. The Muslim League is fortunate that it is starting its action in this holy month."[21]

As the day approached, preparations were made for an all-out war on the streets. In Bengal, where a Muslim League government was in power, special arrangements were made by Premier Suhrawardy to demonstrate the strength of Muslim sentiments about Pakistan. Even before the Muslim League National Council could work out the details of the day, the ministry in Bengal declared 16 August a public holiday against the wishes of the Opposition, the Congress. A mass rally was planned at the foot of the Octerlony Monument near Dalhousie Square in Calcutta, where Suhrawardy, Khwaja Nazimuddin and other League leaders were to speak.

Jinnah's paper, *Dawn*, published from Lahore, came out with a full-page "pledge of sacrifice". The newspaper reiterated: "Today Muslims of India dedicate anew their lives and all they possess to the cause of freedom. Today, let every Muslim swear in the name of Allah to resist aggression," and stated that 'Direct Action' was the only course left for Muslims, because "they offered peace but peace was spurned; they honoured their word but were betrayed; they claimed liberty but are offered thraldom; now might alone can secure their right."[22]

Suhrawardy also held the portfolio of Law and Order. He transferred Hindu police officers from all key posts prior to August 16 and ensured that while twenty-two of the twenty-four police stations had Muslims as in-charge, the remaining two had Anglo-Indians. *Goondas* and bad characters were mobilised by the League from within the city and outside to create trouble. Suhrawardy nonchalantly defended violence in an article he authored in Calcutta's Statesman newspaper stating "bloodshed and disorder are not necessarily evil in themselves, if resorted to for a noble cause"[23].

Tathagata Roy, former Governor and an erudite intellectual of Bengal, vividly describes in his book: "The constables of the Calcutta police were, as a rule, recruited according to what was known as the A.B.C.D. rule – which meant that they were drawn all from the districts of Arrah, Balia, Chhapra and Deoria. These are districts around the boundary of the United Provinces and Bihar, in the area generally known as Bhojpur. People from this area are well-built, tough and loyal – almost ideal police constable material. There was just one problem that Suhrawardy had with them. They were all devout Hindus, and moreover, worshippers of Lord Hanuman, the Hindu God who personifies strength, manliness and undying loyalty to his master, Lord Rama. They, therefore, could not be trusted to carry out the designs that Suhrawardy had in mind.

"In order to get round this problem, Suhrawardy turned to Niaz Mohammed Khan, the ICS officer who, while District Magistrate of Midnapore, had carried out (Bengal Governor) Herbert's nefarious designs of crackdown on the participants in the 'Quit India' movement. The idea was to Muslimise the Calcutta police. Why the Calcutta police in particular? Because Calcutta had already been chosen by the Muslim League as the theatre of the bloodbath that had been scheduled on August 16, 1946, in what they would call 'Direct Action', and what the rest of the world would eventually call the Great Calcutta Killings.

"Niaz Mohammed Khan, under Suhrawardy's orders, journeyed to the northwest to recruit Punjabi Muslim and Pathan constables for the Calcutta police. Pathans are Pashto-speaking Muslim tribesmen inhabiting the barren hills of the frontier, and are divided into a large number of tribes, such as Afridi, Mohmand, Waziri, Khattak, Yusufzai, etc. Blood feuds among between different tribes or different groups (called *khel*) in the same tribe are still very common. These tribes are by nature extremely fierce and cruel – in fact they had been extensively used in British jails in India for application of third-degree methods. Under the benign leadership of Khan Abdul Ghaffar Khan and his Khudai Khidmatgar (Servants of God) party, a considerable number of them had become mellowed and come closer to the Indian mainstream, but this had made little difference to the people away from towns like Peshawar and Kohat. There was another feature that should be mentioned. Because their womenfolk were all kept in strict *purdah*, the Pathans are first cousins of the present-day Afghan Taliban – these rural Pathans had no respect for women, nor were they accustomed to seeing women out in the open. This had some extremely unsavoury consequences."[24]

Calcutta turned into a nightmarish hell on that day by the rioters. Provocative speeches were made at the rally organised by Suhrawardy and other League leaders that afternoon. Over 60,000 to one lakh Muslims were present in the rally.

Muslim League leader Khwaja Nizamuddin, who became the Governor General of Pakistan after Jinnah's death, spoke first. He blamed Hindus for attacking Muslims, forcing the latter to retaliate. Next was the turn of Suhrawardy, who spewed venom. "*Maar ke lenge Pakistan, lad ke lenge Pakistan, le kar rahenge Pakistan, Allahu Akhbar, nara-i-takhbir*" (We will kill and fight to create Pakistan; we are determined to create Pakistan), screamed Suhrawardy.

The cumulative result of these provocations was the carnage that happened on that day and subsequently. Thousands were killed and tens of thousands had to flee Calcutta. The Howrah Bridge was choked with fleeing people.

"Calcutta under mob rule," wrote *Amrit Bazar Patrika* on the next day.[25] Three days later, on August 19, it reported that the city was "strewn with dead bodies", and that the disturbances continued "unabated". Markets were closed, shops that hadn't been looted were shuttered, telephone lines were dead and no transport was available, it reported. The paper commented that there was no way of knowing the actual figures of the dead and the wounded since the city was littered with corpses.

Leaders of the Congress and League, including Nehru

and Jinnah, were largely silent over the Calcutta killings at that time. Nehru was rather dismissive. "Such events as have taken place in Calcutta, deplorable as they are, do not make any major difference to the course of events", he told reporters[26].

In Delhi, Viceroy Wavell was a worried man. He called Nehru and Gandhi to his office and insisted that they should persuade Jinnah to join the interim government before another "Great Calcutta Killings" took place. Jinnah, however, was adamant, and already told Nehru that he wouldn't work under him, whom he once described as a "Peter Pan… who never learns or unlearns anything". When Nehru expressed helplessness in bringing Jinnah into the Government, Wavell indicated that in the absence of a deal between the two parties, he would be compelled to withdraw his invitation to Nehru. Gandhi, normally very pacific, erupted at Wavell's threat. Whatever happened, the Britishers could no longer deprive Indians of their right to decide their fate themselves, he told Wavell. "If India wants her bloodbath, she shall have it", he thundered slapping on Wavell's desk[27].

Some historians, like Patrick French tried to absolve Jinnah of any responsibility for the Calcutta killings. Even Maulana Azad tried to shift the blame on Nehru in his memoirs. "Sixteen August 1946 was a black day not only for Calcutta but for the whole of India… This was one of the greatest tragedies of Indian history and I have to say with the deepest of regret that a large part of the responsibility for this development rests with Jawaharlal. His unfortunate statement that the Congress would be free to modify the Cabinet Mission plan reopened the whole question of political and communal settlement…," he wrote.[28]

But the fact of the matter is that Jinnah was not only aware of the consequences of his war cry, but also wanted Direct Action Day to be that way. He wanted to create an atmosphere of hatred and violence to force the Congress leadership to acquiesce to his demand for Partition.

And the later events proved that Jinnah succeeded. With 'pistol in hand' and violence as the means, he achieved what he could not through negotiations – Pakistan.

Reference—

1. *My Life: Kasturba Gandhi, General Press*
2. *Jinnah-Gandhi Talks (1944). Accessed at https://historypak.com/jinnah-gandhi-talks-1944/*
3. *"Prison Diary" December 28, 1943*
4. *Ibid.*
5. *Jinnah-Gandhi Talks (1944). Accessed at https://historypak.com/jinnah-gandhi-talks-1944/*
6. *Gandhi-Jinnah Talks: Text of Correspondence and Other Relevant Matter, p. 7, The Hindustan Times, New Delhi*
7. *"Jinnah-Gandhi Talks: September 1944: Text of Correspondence and Other Relevant Matter, p. 47, Central Office, All India Muslim League, November 1944*
8. *Where West met East: Einstein, published by AIR Bombay. Accessed at Akashvani, Vol.-XLVII, p. 11, All India Radio Archives, March 14, 1982*
9. *Selected Speeches of Subhas Chandra Bose,pp. 218, Publications Division, Ministry of Information and Broadcasting, Government of India*
10. *Prasad, Rajendra: India Divided, p. 163, Hind Kitabs Ltd.*
11. *Pyarelal (1956): Mahatma Gandhi: The Last Phase: Part 1, p. 314, Navjivan Publishing House, Ahmedabad*
12. *Pyarelal, "Mahatama Gandhi – The Last Phase" pp. 314, Navajivan Publishing House*
13. *Nehru's Press Conference – July 10, 1946. Accessed at http://thepartitionofindia.blogspot.com/2017/06/nehrus-press-conference-july-10-1946.html*
14. *Ibid*
15. *Gopal, Sarvepalli (1976): Jawaharlal Nehru: A Biography, p. 327,*

Oxford University Press, Kolkata

16. *Ibid*
17. *Hayat, Syed Umar: 'The Direct Action Day (1946): Myth and Reality',Pakistan Journal of History and Culture, Vol.-21, p. 1. Accessed at http://www.nihcr.edu.pk/Latest_English_Journal/Pjhc%2021-1,%202000/2-Syed-Umar-Hayat.pdf*
18. *Bourke-White, Margaret: Halfway to Freedom, p. 15, Simon and Schuster, New York*
19. *Akbar, M.J.: Gandhi's Hinduism: The Struggle against Jinnah's Islam, p. 181, Bloomsbury*
20. *Islamic State's Agenda in Bharat – Jihad Manual, Sawt Al-Hind Issues 2 & 3. Accessed at https://hindupost.in/politics/islamic-states-agenda-in-bharat-jihad-manual-sawt-al-hind-issues-2-3/*
21. *Panigrahi, D.N. (2004): India's Partition: The Story of Imperialism in Retreat, p. 300, Routledge*
22. *Sengupta, Debjani: A City of Feeding on Itself: Testimonies and Histories of Direct Action Day, p. 292*
23. *Mosley, Leonard (1965), "The Last Days of the British Raj" pp. 32, Jaico Books*
24. *Roy, Tathagat (2014): The Life and Times of Syama Prasad Mookerjee: A Complete Biography, PrabhatPrakashan*
25. *Amrita Bazaar Patrika, Vol.-LXXVIII, p. 227, August 17, 1946*
26. *Hajari, Nisid (2015), "Midnight's Furies: The Deadly Legacy of India's Partition" pp. 29, Houghton Mifflin Harcourt*
27. *Moon, Penderel (1973), "Wavell: The Viceroy's Journal" pp. 341, Oxford University Press, London*
28. *Azad, Maulana Abul Kalam (1958): India Wins Freedom, p. 137*

□

Unity Discarded General Dethroned

He (Gandhi) had the greatness to embody the oppressed and their sufferings, and to seek truth wherever it might be found. To borrow the famous phrase of Anatole France, "He was a moment in the conscience of mankind".

—Mountbatten

The Direct Action had the desired result on the psyche of the Hindus. Hindu leaders, especially from provinces like Bengal, started demanding Partition of their province into two. The very fact that the same Bengalis were up in arms against the same Partition four decades ago was the testimony to the calamitous failure of the politics during those four decades.

Leadership of the Congress was conspicuous by its silence over the Calcutta killings. Gandhi was at his Sewagram Ashram when the news of the Great Calcutta Killings came. He chose to respond mildly by commenting in *Harijan*, "We are not yet in the midst of civil war. But we are nearing it... If the British are wise, they will keep clear of it."[1]

The civil war that Gandhi was anticipating came soon. At Noakhali in Chittagong, the Muslims unleashed horrendous atrocities against the Hindus in October-November 1946. The violence in Noakhali was not only severer than the one in Calcutta, but it was one-sided too.

Shah Syed Gholam Sarwar Hosseini was a legislator in the Bengal Provincial Assembly between 1937 and 1945 from a radical Left party called the Krishak Sramik Party. He became the leader of the Muslims in Noakhali and Tippera divisions of Chittagong district during those turbulent years. On October 10, 1946, Hosseini called a meeting of the Muslims of Noakhali and delivered a highly provocative speech against the Hindu Mahasabha leaders in particular, and Hindus, in general. That day was an auspicious day of Lakshmi *puja* for the Bengali Hindus. All Hindus were in the midst of celebrations when the attacks began. Hindu localities were besieged by Muslim goons after Hosseini's speech. Hosseini's private army, named Miyar Fauz (army of the Miya), jumped into action. It was hell for the Hindus for the next two months.

The Bengal administration, headed by the 'Butcher of Bengal' Suhrawardy, did not come forward to the help of the Hindus of Noakhali and Tippera until October 15 – a criminal delay of full five days. It also tried to suppress the news from the rest of the country, but soon the horrors of Noakhali reached different parts as the Calcutta-based media started reporting the gory incidents in great detail.

The Statesman on October 16, 1946 reported: "In an area of about 200 sq. miles the inhabitants, surrounded by riotous mobs, are being massacred, their houses being burnt, their womenfolk being forcibly carried away and thousands being subjected to forcible conversion. Thousands of hooligans attacked the villages, compelled them (Hindus) to slaughter their cattle and eat. All places of worship in affected villages have been desecrated. The District Magistrate and the Police Superintendent of Noakhali took no step to prevent it."[2]

Worst victims were the Hindu women. Even Gandhi alluded to it during his visit to Noakhali in early November, where he spent months on to assure that peace returned. When Gandhi was at Calcutta, on his way to Noakhali, an agitated Muslim asked him as to why he had chosen Noakhali first. Was it because the victims were Hindus? More than anything else, Gandhi replied, it was the "cry of the outraged womanhood" that had brought him to Noakhali.[3]

Miss Muriel Leister, member of a relief committee sent to Noakhali, wrote on November 6, 1946: "Worst of all was the plight of women. Several of them had to watch their husbands being murdered and then be forcibly converted and married to some of those responsible for their death. Those women had a dead look. It was not despair, nothing so active as that. It was blackness... the eating of beef and declaration of allegiance to Islam has been forced upon many thousands of women at the price of their lives."[4]

As Nehru became the Prime Minister, Acharya Kripalani, a veteran leader, was elected the president of the Congress Party. Kriplani went to Noakhali ten days after the killings started. In his report submitted to the Congress Working Committee, Kripalani wrote:

"Next morning (October 22, 1946) we visited the interior of one of the affected areas. The place was Charhaim. Charhaim village and the surrounding areas are occupied by Namasudras (Scheduled Castes) numbering about 20,000. It was completely destroyed. Most of the houses were burnt. People were living in sheds, built from the ruins of their houses. All their property had been looted. Cash, ornaments, utensils and clothes, and cattle also, had been taken away by the raiders. All the males and females had only the clothes they were wearing. They had no food to eat. Their condition was pitiable in the extreme. There had been cases of murder, but it was not possible during the short time at our disposal to ascertain the number of the killed. Cases of abduction were reported to us. Even after looting and arson, the villagers were obliged to embrace Islam; they had to perform *'namaz'* and recite the *'kalma'*... All the images of the houses were broken and temples looted and destroyed. The conch-shell bangles of women and vermillion marks, signs of their married life, were removed."[5]

"Not a single rich Muslim house had been looted. To me it appeared to be absolutely communal and absolutely one-sided," he added.[6]

The Congress Working Committee meeting came soon after at Delhi and its resolution on East Bengal contained the following observations: "Reports published in the press and statements of public workers depict a scene of bestiality and medieval barbarity that must fill every decent human being with shame, disgust and anger."[7]

Gandhi went to Noakhali in early November. The violence there had devastated him. Unable to bear it, he wept. "I never experienced such a darkness in my life," he said.[8]

He even started questioning his own methods. "It is a Herculean task that faces me. I am being tested. Is the *satyagraha* of my conception a weapon of the weak, or really that of the strong? I must either realise the latter or lay down my life in the attempt to attain it. That is my quest.

In pursuit of it, I have come to bury myself in this devastated village," he wrote in a letter to the inmates of the Sewagram Ashram.[9]

* * *

As feared, the Noakhali killings had led to a severe reaction in Bihar, where the Hindus and Sikhs had unleashed murder and mayhem against the Muslims and in which a large number of Muslims became the victims.

Earlier, in September, the Interim Government was established in Delhi with Nehru as the Prime Minister. Jinnah initially refused to join the government, but Viceroy Wavell prevailed upon him to join. Surprisingly, despite his sinister role in launching the Direct Action Day and the Great Calcutta Killings, both Nehru and Gandhi were keen that Jinnah joined the Interim Government. Gandhi, although, claimed later, when the interim arrangement failed, that his warnings had come true. "All you may say is that the Interim Government should include the Muslim League representatives. The Congress is prepared to do that," he told Wavell on September 26 in a conversation, as reported by Pyarelal.[10]

Muslim League representatives joined the Interim Government the next day, September 27. The biggest challenge faced by Nehru was to assuage the communal cauldron sweeping across the country due largely to the Direct Action Day misdeeds of the League. But the League members in the government, like Liaquat Ali were more of a hindrance to Nehru and the government's functioning than any help.

"Wavell managed to bring the League into the government but despite Jinnah's assurance of co-operation, his representatives resorted to sabotage from within. In the result, the communal inferno, instead of being extinguished, spread rapidly to various parts of the country with East Bengal, Bihar and Punjab burning with a fury never witnessed before," wrote Rafiq Zakaria.[11]

Helplessness of the Interim Government was witnessed during the Noakhali killings. When Syama Prasad Mookerjee, leader of the Hindu Mahasabha, urged Nehru on October 18 to intervene and help the Hindus of East Bengal since the state police was not protecting them, Nehru used the pretext that law and order was a State Subject, and declined the appeal. However, when riots broke out in Bihar as a reaction to the Noakhali killings and Muslims became the target of the Hindu rage, Nehru immediately proceeded to Patna along with his Cabinet colleague from the Muslim League, Liaquat Ali, and started issuing strong warnings to Hindus. "Some people believe they are taking revenge for atrocities in East Bengal. It was bad enough. Culprits must be punished immediately. The government had to follow such a course by firing machine guns and bombing the people. No government could tolerate such lawlessness," he warned the Hindus and Sikhs of Bihar.[12]

When the news of one hundred Hindus killed in a police firing in Bihar came, Nehru sent a message to Padmaja Naidu saying, "Would you believe it? I was greatly relieved to hear it!"[13]

Nehru's statements came in handy for the League's propaganda of a pogrom against Muslims in India. In November, Dawn published a statement by Jinnah that reiterated his demand of immediate creation of two independent states of Hindustan and Pakistan. He made an important submission in that statement calling for exchange of populations. "The exchange of population will have to be considered seriously as far as possible, especially after this Bihar tragedy", he said[14].

The Interim Government was dysfunctional due to the intransigence and obstructionism of the League members. Nehru, Patel and other Congress members of the government were desperate. They turned to Gandhi again, but Gandhi was committed not to leave Noakhali until peace returned fully. He did not miss to remind his colleagues of his intuition at the time of the Cabinet Mission Plan on whose basis the Interim Government was formed. Nehru and a few members of the Working Committee came to see him at Srirampore and requested him to return to Delhi. Although he didn't agree to leave Noakhali, he did hand over a personal note to Nehru in which he again referred to his suggestion to the Working Committee regarding the Cabinet Mission plan which was ignored. "I suggest frequent consultations with an old, tried servant of the nation,"[15] he wrote, intending to be consulted on all important matters once again.

As the communal carnage continued, the Muslim League's diabolical deeds left the Interim Government paralysed and the Congress leadership flabbergasted. Gandhi continued in Noakhali, living a mud hut, trudging the dusty roads for miles on, day after day, from village to village, "undaunted by hostile reception, offering solace and succour to each and every one of the victims of hate and violence."[16]

* * *

1947, the final year of freedom and Partition, started with British Prime Minister Clement Atlee deciding to replace Wavell with Louis Mountbatten. Mountbatten was a British naval officer and a relative of the royals. While announcing Mountbatten's appointment, Atlee also informed the British Parliament on February 20 that the colonial administration would be withdrawn from India by June 1948. His statement sounded ominous because he insisted that if by then, the Constituent Assembly was not functional due to Muslim League's intransigence and an agreed constitution was not framed, the British Government would consider transferring power to a Central Government or to some provincial governments or in such other ways as may be in the best interests of the Indian people.

It was a complete negation of Cabinet Mission Plan and a definite indication of Partition. Gandhi was most upset. He was hoping that the Congress would reject the proposal after consulting him. Both did not happen; neither was he consulted, nor the Congress opposed the statement. Instead, in the Working Committee meeting held in the first week of March 1947, Congress demanded Partition of Punjab on communal lines. Later, in a press conference at Madras, Kripalani indicated that the same principle could be applied to Bengal also.

Partition of Bengal became the near unanimous demand of the Bengali Hindus after the Noakhali massacre. Hindu Mahasabha leader Syama Prasad Mookerjee was in the forefront of it, but many Congress leaders from Bengal too were demanding the same. But Gandhi was not convinced. Even during his stay at Noakhali, his refrain to the Hindus was that even at the cost of their lives, they shouldn't abandon their Muslim neighbours. He called it as 'courage'.

The news of Congress recommending Partition of

Punjab agitated Gandhi. He was hoping that the Congress leadership would consult him after the note he handed over to Nehru during the latter's visit to Noakhali. He wrote letters, protesting the decision, to both Nehru and Patel. A terse reply came from Patel on March 24. "It was adopted after deepest deliberation. Nothing has been done in a hurry or without full thought," Patel wrote, adding, "it is difficult to explain to you the resolution about the Punjab."[17]

"Such a thing would have been inconceivable in olden days. Even when he (Gandhi) was ranging over the length and breadth of India, they did not fail to consult him before taking any vital decision," writes Pyarelal.[18]

Gandhi returned to Delhi in March. He sought an appointment and met the new Viceroy, Lord Mountbatten on March 31. It was in this meeting, in a final and desperate attempt at preventing the Partition that Gandhi proposed to Jinnah that the transfer of power over entire India could be done to him. There were no takers for the proposal. Nehru and Patel were strongly opposed to it while Jinnah dismissed it as "one of those wily tricks of Gandhi".

By then, the Congress leadership had made up its mind over the eventuality of Partition. The mood in both Punjab and Bengal too had become favourable for Partition. Although leaders like Master Tara Singh were vociferously opposed to the Partition of Punjab, soon they reconciled. In Bengal, the mood was one of urgency. The Hindu members of Bengal in the Central Legislature gave a representation to Mountbatten on April 4, demanding division of their province into East and West Bengal and creation of two separate administrative divisions so that further bloodshed could be avoided.

Gandhi realised that he was no longer wanted in the matters of India's freedom. Not just his *bete noire* Jinnah, but his own close aides, like Nehru and Patel, too no longer supported his thinking. Disillusioned and dejected, he quietly left for Patna to be in the midst of the Muslim victims on April 12.

From there he went to Calcutta on May 8, planning to proceed to Noakhali. Suhrawardy came to see Gandhi with a proposal for united Bengal. Suhrawardy's plan was to have Bengal as the third independent country, besides Hindustan and Pakistan. He even spoke of a "Greater Bengal", which would include parts of Bihar and the whole of Assam province[19]. In that he was supported by some Hindu leaders, like Sarat Chandra Bose, but Syama Prasad Mookerjee and others were not in favour. Surprisingly, Gandhi took a softer stand towards Suhrawardy's proposal. "...if you would retain Bengal for the Bengalis – Hindus and Mussalmans – intact by non-violent means, I am quite willing to act as your honorary private secretary and live under your roof," he told Suhrawardy.[20]

No wonder the Hindus were upset with Gandhi one more time. Luckily, Nehru and Patel didn't accept this proposal. So, it went nowhere.

* * *

Things started moving fast while Gandhi was away. In April, Mountbatten held the meeting of all the British Governors, where a plan for transfer of power was discussed. Lord Ismay, Mountbatten's Chief of Staff was assigned the responsibility of drafting it. Initially the Indian leadership was kept in the dark about it. The plan, called as the DICKIE Bird Plan, was taken to London by Ismay for approval of the British Cabinet. Under this plan, the British Government would grant the option to all the eleven provinces of the British India and 559 princely states of joining either India or Pakistan or remaining independent.

Atlee's government gave its accent to the proposal. However, when Mountbatten placed the proposal before Nehru, he rejected it in toto. V.P. Menon, Secretary of the States Department in the government, was the only Indian civil servant in Mountbatten's staff at that time. Mountbatten entrusted him with the responsibility of redrafting the Bill after consulting Nehru.

"... the then Secretary of State's Department, V.P. Menon... advised that power be transferred to two independent British dominions, India and Pakistan. This was opposed by Mohammed Ali Jinnah, who wanted referendum in the North-West Frontier Province (N-WFP) and Baluchistan. V.P. Menon had suggested that Mountbatten give an assurance to Nehru and Sardar Patel that Britain would oppose the princely states becoming independent, and instead persuade them to join either of the two new nation-states (which would ensure that 90 per cent of them would join India) in exchange for Congress support of a fresh 'reference to the electorate' in the NWFP and Baluchistan. In less than half a day, this new plan was adopted by Mountbatten and presented to Nehru, who was much more receptive. However, in the process, he was successful in getting the proposal dearest to Britain accepted, which meant dominion status for India and Pakistan and the separation of Baluchistan and NWFP from India and giving that to Pakistan," writes R.K. Kaushik, former Chief Secretary of Punjab in an article in *The Tribune.*[21]

The new proposal was ready by early May and Mountbatten himself took it to London this time for approval. He returned to India on May 31 with Atlee's approval and immediately called the meeting of various Indian leaders on June 2. Nehru, Patel and Kripalani were there from the Congress, while Jinnah, Liaquat and Nishtar represented the League. Sardar Baldev Singh was also called.

Once Mountbatten was successful in convincing these leaders, he did not waste time. He immediately called a press conference and announced the plan of Partition of India. The plan, which had the final stamp of approval by the Congress for the Partition of India, came to be known as the "June 3rd Plan".

The June 3rd Plan entailed the following provisions:

- Partition of British India into two dominions of India and Pakistan.
- Partition of Bengal and Punjab into two parts and giving to the two dominions.
- Termination of British suzerainty over the princely states with the option for them of choosing to join either of the dominions or remaining independent.
- Conducting a referendum in NWFP and Baluchistan.

The 'June 3rd Plan' was a surrender by the Congress leadership before Mountbatten, who was sent by Atlee with the instruction that the country be split between Hindus and Muslims as soon as possible. Atlee's declared timeline for the transfer of power was June 1948. However, Mountbatten decided to advance it by ten months to August 15, 1947.

In their eagerness to get rid of the League menace

quickly and occupy power without hassles, the Congress leaders agreed to a compromise formula that would haunt them for years to come. It was a hurriedly drawn plan. It was unequal and unjust in the sense that NWFP, a region that had been loyal to the Congress under the leadership of Khan Abdul Ghaffar Khan, was given away to Pakistan in the name of referendum. Similarly, the Congress leadership had agreed for similar referendum in the Sylhet district of Assam, which too eventually ended up in Pakistan's hands. Sadly, no such referendum was sought for Hindu or non-Muslim-majority areas inside Pakistan, like the Chittagong Hill Tracts or cities like Karachi, Lahore and Hyderabad. As a result, all those areas went to Pakistan.

Partition involved demarcation of the boundaries on two sides – west and east – a total of over 7,000 kms. It was undertaken in a hurried manner by a person who had no experience of India until then. Cyril Radcliffe, a barrister by profession from London Bar, was given the responsibility of drawing the Partition lines of Bengal and Punjab and delineating the remaining border between the two dominions. Time he got was just two months. Needless to say, the exercise was full of blunders, the price for which was to be paid by the innocent civilians – Hindu, Sikh and Muslim – on both sides.

Jinnah had made full use of the concessions. Iskander Mirza, the great grandson of Mir Jafar, the traitor of the Battle of Plassey in 1757, was entrusted with the job of launching a *jihad* to win the referendum in NWFP by Jinnah. Mirza was later rewarded with the presidentship of Pakistan for delivering NWFP to the League.

"It can be summed up that seldom any 'plan' in history

had such a walloping, nay humungous and searing, effect on humanity as the June 3rd Plan had because it led to the migration of more than 13 million people, savage death to a million innocents, overnight forcible change of religion of about 2 lakh and kidnapping of about 80,000 women," wrote Kaushik.[22]

Like before, Gandhi was not taken into confidence by the Congress leadership in this matter too; he was only informed. But Gandhi did not oppose the plan. He, instead tried to suggest that nobody should be blamed for it. He said that his message to the Congress was that they shouldn't yield even an inch to "force" and the Congress leaders had told him that they were yielding not to any "force", but to "circumstances". He wouldn't find Viceroy Mountbatten to be responsible either, for any wrongdoing. He tried his best to keep India united, but both Congress and League wanted it divided. He tried his best to impress upon them to stick to the Cabinet Mission Plan, but he failed. He was a servant of the Congress because he was the servant of India. He could not be disloyal to it. He admonished the socialists who came to him with the demand that he should lead the opposition to the Partition.

Gandhi received enough opprobrium from various sections, which included criticism, ridicule and even abuse. A man wedded to truth, Gandhi's response somehow lacked spirit. He had once declared that Partition was a sin and it should happen only over his dead body. "Why then was he silent?" asked a person. Gandhi responded by saying that when he made the statement, he was voicing the public opinion. But when the public opinion was against him, was he to coerce it? Another taunted him by asking why wouldn't he undertake a fast unto death? Gandhi's reply was that he "could not fast at the dictation of anyone. Such fasts could not be lightly undertaken. They could conceivably be wholly undesirable. The fasts could not be undertaken out of anger. Anger was a short madness. He must, therefore, undertake the fast only when the still small voice within him called for it."[23]

Gandhi had undertaken many fasts during his three decades in India. He undertook a major fast to convince Dr. Ambedkar to give up the demand for separate electorates for the depressed classes. But when Congress was surrendering before the machinations of the League and the British, his inner voice didn't call him for any drastic action.

When Atlee gave the reasons for leaving India, his main emphasis was that India had become ungovernable due to the revolt in the Royal Indian Navy and the Air Force. Outgoing Viceroy Wavell had already warned the government in London that if it continued to held on to India against its will and the well-organised liberation movement, it would become "a running sore which would sap the strength of the British Empire"[24].

But Gandhi had a different take. He insisted that the British had decided to leave India because of his non-violence. He met Viceroy Mountbatten on June 6 and addressed a prayer meeting after returning. He told the assembled members in that prayer meeting that "the Viceroy had frankly told him that his one object was to withdraw from India in the quickest manner possible, leaving behind peace and order throughout India. They had decided to go in June 1948 but now they would probably withdraw by August 15, this year. Why had they decided to go? They were impressed by our non-violent struggle. India believed that the British rule was an evil, yet she did not try to kill the British. India simply tried to non-cooperate with the evil, not with the evildoer. Such interval, as was necessary, was due to the fact that it was a voluntary withdrawal."[25]

Although all his efforts failed and the country was subjected to brutal Partition, Gandhi stuck to his guns on several of his pet themes. At another prayer meeting address on June 12, he dwelt at length, rather unconvincingly, on why India shouldn't be called Hindustan. Muslims cannot become a separate nation if the non-Muslims do not respond, he made an argument, indirectly hinting that Hindus too considered Muslims as separate. "Hindustan will mean the abode only of Hindus," he inferred, and hence rejected the suggestion by some.

"The Muslim-majority areas may call themselves Pakistan, but the rest and the largest part of India need not call itself Hindustan. In contradistinction to Pakistan, it will mean the abode of the Hindus. Do the Hindus feel so? Have the Parsees, the Christians and Jews born in India and the Anglo-Indians who do not happen to have the white skin, any other home than India? I will omit the Muslims for the time being. I suppose such is the reason why Jawaharlalji refuses to call the non-Pakistan areas as Hindustan and loves to call them by the proud name of the Union of Indian Republics, from which some Muslim-majority areas have seceded. History has shown that the possession of proud names does not make the possessors great. Men and groups are known not by what they call themselves but by their deeds," he admonished them.[26]

Talking about the language, Gandhi reverted to his position of 1920s and insisted, "I am told that there are people in the Union who have wrongly come to the conclusion that now there is no occasion for Hindustani, a compatible mixture of Hindi and Urdu. There are many holy shrines of Islam. Will they be honoured equally with the others? Will it be the same with the Muslim seats of learning? On the proper treatment of these and such other questions depends the real unity of India and I say this irrespective of what is said or done in Pakistan."[27]

* * *

The Congress Committee meeting held on June 14-15 was stormy. Many seniors were dejected and angry. There was talk of open defiance. When Govind Ballabh Pant moved the resolution supporting June 3rd Plan, several stalwarts rose to oppose it. P.D. Tandon and Khan Abdul Ghaffar Khan were prominent among those who opposed the Plan and the capitulation of the Congress leadership before the British. Tandon argued that rather than paying such a heavy price, the nation should have been made to endure the sufferings at the hands of the British for some more time.

Ghaffar Khan, also known as 'Frontier Gandhi', was heartbroken. He wept on the podium asking why the sturdy Pathans, who had fought for freedom in a united India under the leadership of Gandhi, were being subjected to this punishment. "You have thrown us to the wolves; which Muslims, who joined you, will ever trust you?", he agonizingly asked. Gandhi got up from his place, placed his arms around the weeping Khan and took him away.

Later, Ghaffar Khan authored his autobiography, originally in Pashto and later translated into English as *My Life and Struggle*, in which he presented a different first-person account. While Gandhi opposed the use of the word "Hindustan", Khan stuck to that word. While Gandhi argued that the British had agreed to leave India because of his non-violent movement, Khan insisted that, on the contrary, it was the bravery and struggles of the Pathans in support of the cause of Hindustan that the British had gone away. "The Congress had been waging the struggle for the liberation of Hindustan for the past sixty years, but the British, let alone total Independence, had not even granted them limited freedom. But when the Pukhtuns joined them in this struggle and gave sacrifices in Qissa Khwani, Takar, Uthmanzai, Kohat, Hathikhel, and Mirwais; and in similar fashion our tribal brothers allied themselves with the Pukhtuns and waged a *jihad* for the liberation of Hindustan, and bared their chests as shields to the guns and tanks of the British and stood firm like a mountain before their onslaughts, only then were the British compelled to agree to the Independence of Hindustan," he wrote.[28]

Ghaffar Khan did not blame Gandhi directly but sought to apportion blame on Sardar Patel. "Mountbatten was a very intelligent and far-sighted man. He would find out what his Hindustani companions were feeling in their hearts. When he realised that Sardar Patel was prepared to accept his plan of Partition of Hindustan, then, to bring him on board, he used the full potential of the power of his personality, charm and deceit. In his discussions, he would compare Sardar Patel to a walnut; his exterior was hard, but when broken, the interior emerged soft. After the conquest of Sardar Patel, he turned his attention to Jawaharlal. Initially, Jawaharlal would not entertain any thought of Partition and his reaction would be very strong. But Mountbatten pursued him until, gradually, the strength of his opposition to the idea broke down," he wrote.[29]

"I was very saddened. This was because we considered this not so much as the partitioning of Hindustan, as that of the Muslims. I was, from the beginning, of the view, and I still believe, that the Cabinet Mission Plan was the best solution for the Muslims in every respect. It would have ensured the unity of Hindustan and also provided each community the opportunity for a free and respectable existence," he said.[30]

He angrily reacted to the "infidelity of the Congress" and said: "We had allied with the Congress in the struggle for freedom on the condition that we would jointly liberate the country and free ourselves of the yoke of slavery. But when the time came, all the promises made to us were discarded, and nobody asked us about our future. Instead, the referendum about opting to join Pakistan or Hindustan was forced down our throats and we were treated as pawns and bargained away in this deal. The sacrifices were given by us, our blood was shed, our properties and wealth were ruined, and the benefits went to others," he bemoaned.[31] Khan alleged that the leaders of the Congress, who used to consult him on all important matters, did not only not consult him, but not even informed him. "I am annoyed over the fact that even the Congress Working Committee showed no sympathy or extend any help to us. They tied us by the feet and hands and handed us over to the Muslim League," he cried out from his heart.[32]

"The Congress leaders said that the conditions were such that there was no other way, other than Partition. But who created these conditions? They themselves are responsible for them. If they had not partitioned Hindustan, then Hindustan and the Hindus would not have experienced such bloodshed," he wrote.[33]

After Ghaffar Khan's and others' speeches, amidst growing resentment over the decision taken by Nehru, Patel and others over Partition, Gandhi rose and addressed the delegates at the Congress session. By then he understood the mood in the session. He started his address gently, without displaying any emotions. He was also opposed to the Partition and had done whatever was in his hands to prevent it, he told them. He blamed the "circumstances" for his defeat. "But I do not find that strength in us today. If you had it, I would also be with you and if I felt strong enough myself, I would, alone, take up the flag of revolt," he told them. But then, he declared that he was helpless. "Sometimes, certain decisions, however unpalatable they might be, had to be taken. The members of the Working Committee are old and tried leaders. It would be unwise, if not impossible, to remove them at this juncture. Out of evil, sometimes good came out. Rama was exiled because of his father's fault but ultimately his exile resulted in the defeat of Ravana," he contended before the audience.[34]

Gandhi had argued on the same lines a few days earlier when the socialist leaders came to him, protesting against the decision of Partition. He could not convince them. But the tempers in the Congress session had certainly cooled down. When an enthusiastic member came to him and said, "Gandhiji, at last our non-violent army has won against the powerful British," Gandhi wryly responded by saying, "Yes, but it has also defeated and dethroned its General."[35]

Reference—

1. *Gandhi, M.K.: September 15, 1946, Harijan, vol. X, No. 32*
2. *Davis, Ashlyn (2021): Noakhali Riots, October 10, 1946: Organised Muslim mobs attacked, raped and slaughtered thousands of Hindu*

Bengalis." Accessed at https://www.jihadwatch.org/2021/10/noakhali-riots-october-10-1946-organized-muslim-mobs-attacked-raped-and-slaughtered-thousands-of-hindu-bengalis

3. Zakaria, Rafiq (1999): Gandhi and the Break-up of India, p. 212, Bharatiya Vidya Bhavan
4. Nagarkar, V. V. (1975): Genesis of Pakistan, p. 446, Allied Publishers
5. Noakhali 1946. Accessed at https://noakhali1946.blogspot.com/2011/08/noakhali-riots-truth-sacrificed.html
6. Ibid
7. Ibid
8. Zakaria, Rafiq (1999): Gandhi and the Break-up of India, p. 213, Bharatiya Vidya Bhavan
9. Tendulkar, D.G.: Mahatma, p. 320, Bombay K. Jhaveri and D.G. Tendulkar
10. Pyarelal (1956): Mahatma Gandhi: The Last Phase: Part 1, p. 274, Navjivan Publishing House, Ahmedabad
11. Zakaria, Rafiq (1999): Gandhi and the Break-up of India, p. 211, Bharatiya Vidya Bhavan
12. Noakhali, 1946. Accessed at https://noakhali1946.blogspot.com/2011/08/noakhali-riots-truth-sacrificed.html
13. "Selected Works of Jawaharlal Nehru" Vol. 1, pp. 65, Ed. By S. Gopal, Jawaharlal Nehru Memorial Fund
14. Moon, Penderel (1970), "The Transfer of Power 1942-47" pp. 73-75, H.M. Stationery Office
15. Tendulkar, D.G.: Mahatma: Vol.-VII, p. 401, Bombay K. Jhaveri and D.G. Tendulkar
16. Zakaria, Rafiq (1999): Gandhi and the Break-up of India, p. 219, Bharatiya Vidya Bhavan
17. Pyarelal (1956): Mahatma Gandhi: The Last Phase: Part 1, p. 35, Navjivan Publishing House, Ahmedabad
18. Ibid
19. Ahmed, Ishtiaq (2020), "Jinnah: His Successed, Failures and Role in History" pp. 65, Penguin
20. Pyarelal (1956): Mahatma Gandhi: The Last Phase: Part 1, p. 35, Navjivan Publishing House, Ahmedabad
21. Kaushi, R.K. (2018): Remembering Mountbatten's June 3 Plan. Accessed at https://www.tribuneindia.com/news/archive/comment/remembering-mountbatten-s-june-3-plan-599572
22. Ibid
23. Tendulkar, D.G.: Mahatma, Vol.-VII, p. 09, Bombay K. Jhaveri and D.G. Tendulkar

24. *Moon, Penderel (1973), "Wavell: The Viceroy's Journal" pp. 330, Oxford University Press, London*
25. *Tendulkar, D.G.: Mahatma, Vol.-VII, p. 10, Bombay K. Jhaveri and D.G Tendulkar*
26. *Ibid*
27. *Ibid*
28. *Khan, Abdul Ghaffar (2021): The Great Betrayal. Aaccessed at https://openthemagazine.com/essays/the-great-betrayal/*
29. *Ibid*
30. *Ibid*
31. *Ibid*
32. *Ibid*
33. *Ibid*
34. *Zakaria, Rafiq (1999): Gandhi and the Break-up of India, p. 230, Bharatiya Vidya Bhavan*
35. *Zakaria, Rafiq (1999): Gandhi and the Break-up of India, p. 231, Bharatiya Vidya Bhavan*

□

Conclusion

I have never, even in my drea, thought that I was Mahatma and that others were Alpatma (little soul)

—Gandhi

Three major Partitions happened in the world in the second half of the 1940s. Germany was partitioned into the eastern and western blocs in 1945, followed by India into Hindustan and Pakistan in 1947. Finally, Israel was created by partitioning Palestine in 1948.

Germany's partition was temporary. The Berlin Wall, constructed in the early 1960s to accord permanence to it, was dismantled by the Germans in less than three decades. The country was reunified in 1989. But in India and Palestine, Partition was a terrible affair, leading to a full-scale war in Israel and a mass migration accompanied by mind-numbing violence in India.

The Arab-Israel war at the time of the partition of Palestine in 1947-49 caused the death of over 30,000 people by some estimates. More than the war, the run up to the formation of Israel had seen much greater violence, which is famously known as 'holocaust'. Hitler's Nazi Army had unleashed an unheard-of bestiality over the innocent Jews all across Europe that was captured by it. The Israeli and other historians have estimated the number of Jews killed in the death camps during the holocaust to be over six million.

The death and destruction caused at the time of India's Partition were no less horrifying. More than a million were murdered, while many millions more had to endure a treacherous migration across the hastily created border, often on foot. Hundreds of thousands could not make it, as they were waylaid and butchered. Historian William Dalrymple estimates the numbers to be more than fifteen million people uprooted, and between one and two million dead.

Those horrors of Partition are difficult to forget. Dalrymple, in an article in *New Yorker*, quotes from a book by Nisid Hajari, *Midnight's Furies*, about the brutality of the period: "Gangs of killers set whole villages aflame, hacking to death men and children and the aged while carrying off young women to be raped. Some British soldiers and journalists who witnessed the Nazi death camps claimed Partition's brutalities were worse: pregnant women had their breasts cut off and babies hacked out of their bellies; infants were found literally roasted on spits."[1]

Dalrymple says that the comparison with the death camps was not so far-fetched as it may seem. He quotes the Pakistani historian Ayesha Jalal, who called the Partition "the central historical event in twentieth-century South Asia", and wrote, "A defining moment that is neither beginning nor end, Partition continues to influence how the peoples and states of postcolonial South Asia envisage their past, present and future."[2]

The Partition of India was a meaningless and reckless act. Across the border, for Saadat Hasan Manto, the famed author, it was all sheer madness. Those women raped, with bulged stomachs, distressed him. "What will happen to those bellies – would the offspring belong to Pakistan or India?"[3] Manto questioned in innocent grief. His dark satire on Partition-time madness, 'Toba Tek Singh', ends with his eponymous hero Tek Singh seen stranded on no-man's land between the newly created India and Pakistan. "On one side, behind barbed wire, stood together the lunatics of India and on the other side, behind more barbed wire, stood the lunatics of Pakistan. In between, on a bit of earth which had no name, lay Toba Tek Singh," Manto provocatively demurs.[4]

Partition was not inevitable even until the early 1940s. But then, the British were in a hurry to leave. Louis Mountbatten arrived in India in March 1947 with the mandate to free the country before June 1948. After meeting Mohammad Ali Jinnah, "a psychopathic case", Mountbatten decided not to wait for that long. In June, he unilaterally declared that the British would Partition India and leave in less than three months.

Gandhi could not reconcile to the fact that a "maniac" and "an evil genius" like Jinnah could have his way, while there was nobody among his disciples to stand by him. He retreated to Bengal to attend to the victims of the bigotry and brutality of its rabid communalist premier, Hussain Suhrawardy. Jawaharlal Nehru, who once called Partition "fantastic nonsense", reconciled quickly and declared in April 1947, "I want that those who stand as an obstacle in our way should go their own way."[5] In India, Rajendra Babu became the first President of partitioned India and Nehru its first Prime Minister. In Pakistan, Manto was branded a traitor and thrown into jail and died a broken man in 1955, at the age of forty-two.

* * *

For the Hindus, Partition was not merely a loss of territory; it was the vivisection of their revered motherland. The urge for undoing it and reclaiming that lost territory, Akhand Bharat, remains a fervent dream for many of them, as Israel remained for the Jews for over two millennia.

The partition of Germany was rejected by people on both sides of the Berlin Wall. They pulled it down and ended the colonial game. Both the last Prime Minister of East Germany, Lothar de Maizière, and the leader of Opposition, Richard Schröder stood by their people. Despite domestic opposition in the Soviet Union, Mikhail Gorbachev demonstrated statesmanship by not interfering.

Unfortunately, the Partition of India was not just about land, but about minds. The premise was that Hindus and Muslims cannot live together. Jinnah, who was once hailed as 'the Ambassador of Hindu-Muslim Unity' and had disparagingly dismissed the propaganda about Hindu domination as just "a bogey, put before you (Muslims) by your enemies to frighten you", turned the tables by the 1940s and maniacally argued that they could never live together. He won.

Jinnah and Gandhi were two opposite poles in this saga of four decades. And their journeys too were in opposite directions. Jinnah began his political career as a nationalist. He once said that he wanted to become 'Muslim Gokhale'. On his part, Gokhale described him as the "best ambassador of Hindu-Muslim unity". But in three decades' time, Jinnah became just the opposite of what he was. He became the wrecker of Indian unity and did everything possible to wean away Muslims from the Indian society. From someone committed to Hindu-Muslim unity, Jinnah became the ardent believer that Hindus and Muslims can never live together.

Gandhi moved in the opposite direction. He had himself confessed about his obsession with Hindu-Muslim unity when he entered the Congress in 1915. He cultivated a generation of Muslim leaders at a time when there were only a handful of Muslims, like Badruddin Tyabji and Maulana Azad in Congress. But, as he witnessed the direction that the Muslim leadership, especially Jinnah took, he realised that he was chasing a mirage. In the last eight years, after the Lahore resolution of the League, Gandhi became more and more obsessed with preserving the unity of India rather than the unity of the Congress and the League. In that effort, he went to the extent of offering Jinnah the leadership of the entire country and submitting to Suhrawardy that he would work as his secretary if only he were ready to keep Bengal united. Gandhi failed.

Louis Fischer, who authored the best-selling book, *The Life of Mahatma Gandhi* after spending many hours interviewing Gandhi, highlights the fact that Gandhi had rejected all the three British offers of transfer of power: Cripps Mission in 1942, the Cabinet Mission in 1946, and the Mountbatten Plan in 1947. He called the Mountbatten Plan "a wooden loaf", difficult to eat and impossible to digest. All this was because of Gandhi's "devotion to the idea of a united India," Fischer writes.

While analysing the developments leading to Partition, we often make the mistake of blaming Gandhi for all the sins and finding virtues in Jinnah that don't exist. In his lifetime, Gandhi had endured so much hate. Birla House, where he was staying, was attacked by Hindu and Sikh refugees when he forced the Nehru government to release 55 crore rupees to the newly formed government of Pakistan. They would have succeeded in causing physical harm to him had police not intervened and *lathi*-charged them. They shouted slogans, like "Death to Gandhi", provoking Nehru to sprint towards them and challenge them to kill him. Finally, Gandhi died at the hands of a hardline Hindu who believed that Gandhi was harming the interests of the Hindus and Hindustan.

It is a travesty that Jinnah, a non-practicing, and perhaps non-believing Muslim, became the Father of Pakistan. He died a natural death, but Gandhi, a Sanatani Hindu, blamed by Jinnah and the Muslim League of Hinduising politics, died at the hands of a Hindu. Seven decades after his death, in the eyes of a section of the Hindus, Gandhi continues to remain anti-Hindu appeaser of the Muslims responsible for the Partition of India.

Was he anti-Hindu? At the Second Round Table Conference in London, when he was described as a leader of the Hindus, Gandhi firmly rejected that introduction. "Not Hindu", he said firmly[6]. But that was only in the context of the mischievous British efforts at dividing Indian society on caste and religious lines and branding Congress as merely a body of the Hindus. Otherwise, Gandhi was never apologetic about his religious beliefs and convictions. He declared in Young India in 1924 that "My patriotism is subservient to my religion"[7]. In an earlier article in Young India, he explained the reasons for considering himself as a Sanatani Hindu. They were: his acceptance of the scriptures like the Vedas, Upanishads etc as valid, his belief in Dharma, his acceptance of idol worship and his devotion to cow-protection[8]. "Every fibre of my being is Hindu", he wrote in Young India in 1924[9].

Gandhi was accused by the Muslims, including Jinnah, of Hinduising the Congress, but a section of the Hindus accused him of anti-Hindu policies. When he went to Bihar to tell the Hindus and Sikhs not to indulge in revenge and retaliation, some were angry and accused him of sympathising with the Muslims. "How could you ever think like that?" he asked in agony with tears in his eyes, "I am proud to be a Hindu. I have lived and will die for Hinduism. Every fibre of my being is Hindu. To say that I do not care for Hindus is the worst travesty of truth."[10]

He spent months in Noakhali vowing not to go back until the Muslims accorded full protection to the Hindus there. He went to the refugee camps in Delhi, where he occasionally faced some opposition, and personally enquired about the well-being of the Hindus and Sikhs living there. He saw the Rashtriya Swayamsevak Sangh (RSS) volunteers working there. He called the RSS "a well-organised and well-disciplined body".

Was Gandhi an appeaser? Yes. In the initial decades of his politics in India, he tried to imitate his South African model here. But, unlike in India, the struggle in South Africa was essentially between the British colonial rulers and the immigrant peoples – both Hindus and Muslims. There the fight was essentially about securing rights, like equality and dignity. Gandhi's contribution to that struggle was enormous. Out of the seed he had sown emerged the tree called Nelson Mandela. Mandela faced the challenge that Gandhi faced in India, in a different way.

In South Africa, rugby was the national game of the White people, while the Black Africans played football. The Black Africans, although loved rugby, saw in it the symbol of oppression. Mandela, after his release from prison after seventeen harsh years, and after becoming President of the country, decides to convert rugby, a symbol of hate and apartheid, into the symbol of unity of the African nation. He meets the captain of the all-White rugby team, Francois Pienaar ahead of the World Cup at Durban, and asks him to use the game to end divisions in the country between the Blacks and the Whites. He calls upon his people to support the team.

Many Black Africans, including Winnie, Mandela's wife, were angry at him. But Mandela told them one thing: "You elected me to lead; now let me lead". He appeared at the stadium when the African team played the final against New Zealand. When it won during extra time, the 65,000 African audience erupted in jubilation. They chanted "Nelson, Nelson, Nelson". The country was never the same after that.

"I could never reach the standard of morality, simplicity and love for the poor set by the Mahatma," said Mandela while delivering a speech in 1993 at the inaugural ceremony of the Gandhi Memorial in South Africa. "The Mahatma is an integral part of our history because it is here that he first experimented with truth; here that he demonstrated his characteristic firmness in pursuit of justice; here that he developed *satyagraha* as a philosophy and a method of struggle," he added.[11]

Gandhi innocently believed that the same methods would work in India too. But the Indian situation was different. Here, those fighting against the British were not any immigrants, nor were they merely asking for some rights; they were demanding freedom as a birth right, as Tilak would put it, or as a fundamental aspiration, as

Aurobindo calls it. Gandhi did realise it, but by then it was late – late not because Jinnah had hardened his position by then, but because his own comrades had abandoned Gandhi.

Nehru, whom Gandhi once affectionately called as "our Englishman"[12] was a believer in 'freedom at all costs' philosophy in his younger days. He had disagreements with Gandhi when the latter insisted on the purity of both means and ends. As the freedom movement reached its goal, Nehru included Partition also as one of the costs. He tried to give a philosophical twist to it in a speech in August 1947, saying "Division is better than a union of unwilling hearts"[13]. He also claimed that "great events were underway" and some of that greatness fell on men like him and Jinnah[14]. So did the other leaders, the "tired old men, hungry for power", as Ram Manohar Lohia put it.

In 1956, Nehru told Michael Brecher, his biographer, that the Congress leadership agreed to Partition because they found that as the only solution to end violence. They were also not agreeable to the Cabinet Mission Plan, which could have ensured a united India, but left the central government weak. In 1960, he confessed to British journalist Leonard Mosley that they were "tired of arguing with Jinnah and considered that Partition was most likely to be a temporary arrangement"[15].

Gandhi was a shattered man when Partition was announced. "My life's work seems to be over. I hope God will spare me further humiliation,"[16] he bemoaned, pleading in agony, "I shall perhaps not be alive to witness it but should the evil I apprehended overtake India and her Independence be imperilled, let posterity know what agony this old soul went through thinking of it. Let it not be said that Gandhi was a party to India's vivisection."[17]

Gandhi may not be fully absolved of the sequence of events that had ended in the tragic Partition of the country, but it would be unfair to put the entire blame on one man who represented many lofty ideals and inspired generations. Gandhi was like a mystic and a metaphysical idealist.

During the final years of Partition, many foreign correspondents used to visit Gandhi at his Ashram in Wardha. For most of them, it was unbelievable that the great freedom movement of India was being run from that "snake-infested backwater".

"Wardha had few charms. The water was polluted. Malaria was widespread, and the sticky, oppressive heat killed many people annually", wrote an American journalist[18].

Sitting in the mud and thatch hut, "a cross between a third-rate raunch and a refugee camp" was the frail old man Gandhi, shaking up the mighty British Empire. He probably belonged to a different time and space. In 1929, Jinnah called Gandhi's policies "utterly unsuited to modern times and the realities we have to face in India"[19]. Those words proved more prophetic after Congress accepted the June 3rd Plan. The Congress leaders had not only rejected Gandhi's life idea of united India but also his life ideal of moral politics.

Gandhi was a man of convictions. Once he offered to Viceroy Linlithgow that he could go and speak to Hitler. He wrote an open letter "To Every Briton" in July 1940 asking them not to fight Hitler and Mussolini and let them have what they wanted. "Britons should lie down and die as heroes of non-violence and then the war would be over", he advised[20].

He gave a similar advise to the Bengali Hindus to "die fearlessly" at the hands of their neighbors without fighting back. "There will be no tears but only joy if tomorrow I get the news that all three of you (have been) killed", he told a trio of his Bengali followers who were going to the region on a mercy mission[21].

He urged the women of Noakhali to remember "the incomparable power of Sita"[22]. He advised them to commit suicide rather than submit to the Muslim hooligans; they should "learn how to die before a hair of their head could be injured". They could "suffocate themselves or... bite their tongues to end their lives". If such methods were difficult, they should drink poison, he advised. "His idea was not an idle idea. He meant all he said", reads Gandhi's own transcript of his comments[23].

His Saint-like innocence was misunderstood by many and many found inconsistency in his words and deeds. But Gandhi had his explanation for that. "My aim is not to be consistent with my previous statements on a given question, but to be consistent with truth as it may present itself to me at a given moment. The result is that I have grown from truth to truth", he confessed[24].

Gandhi was an enigma to many in his life time. He continues to evoke strong sentiments and resentment even to this day. His Bhakts elevate him to a super human moral pedestal while his critics evaluate him from a contemporary religio-political lens. Gandhi probably lived somewhere in between these two levels.

"More than anything, though, my fascination with India had to do with Mahatma Gandhi. Along with (Abraham) Lincoln, (Martin Luther) King and (Nelson) Mandela, Gandhi had profoundly influenced my thinking. As a young man, I'd studied his writings and found him giving voice to some of my deepest instincts," former US President Barak Obama stated in his memoir, *A Promised Land*.[25] "His notion of '*satyagraha*', or devotion to truth, and the power of non-violent resistance to stir the conscience; his insistence on our common humanity and the essential oneness of all religions; and his belief in every society's obligation, through its political, economic and social arrangements, to recognise the equal worth and dignity of all people – each of these ideas resonated with me. Gandhi's actions had stirred me even more than his words; he'd put his beliefs to the test by risking his life, going to prison, and throwing himself fully into the struggles of his people," he wrote.[26]

M.S. Golwalkar, the Sarsanghachalak of the RSS, who was wrongfully imprisoned by the Nehru government after Gandhi's murder, said in 1949, "If Gandhism is 'reactionary' in that it wants to revive the highest human values, we have no objection to be bracketed with Gandhiji as 'reactionaries'."[27]

Probably India did not deserve a Gandhi at that time. He was perhaps ahead of his times. Gokhale, whom Gandhi declared as his 'political guru' in 1915, was right in describing Gandhi on different occasions as "Indomitable..., made of the stuff of which great heroes and martyrs are made, immortal, a more exalted spirit has never moved on this earth".

Reference—

1. *Dalrymple, William (2015): The Great Divide. Accessed at https://www.newyorker.com/magazine/2015/06/29/the-great-divide-books-dalrymple*
2. *Ibid*
3. *Pillai, Manu S. (2017): Saadat Hasan Manto and Partition's Children. Accessed at https://www.livemint.com/Leisure/gSfXrOk4EpQXWLw1w5fzzO/Saadat-Hasan-Manto-and-partitions-*

children.html

4. *Manto, Saadat Hasan (1998): Toba Tek Singh. Accessed at http://www.sacw.net/partition/tobateksingh.html*
5. *Dalrymple, William (2015): The Great Divide. Accessed at https://www.newyorker.com/magazine/2015/06/29/the-great-divide-books-dalrymple*
6. *Fischer, Louis (1997), "The Life of Mahatama Gandhi" pp. 364, Harper Collins*
7. *Gandhi, M.K. "The Collected Works of Mahatama Gandhi" Vol. 23, pp. 5, Gandhi Sevagram Ashram*
8. *Gandhi, M.K. "The Collected Works of Mahatama Gandhi" Vol. 24, pp. 370, Gandhi Sevagram Ashram*
9. *Gandhi, M.K. "The Collected Works of Mahatama Gandhi" Vol. 29, pp. 212, Gandhi Sevagram Ashram*
10. *Zakaria, Rafiq (1999): Gandhi and the Break-up of India, p. 258, Bharatiya Vidya Bhavan*
11. *Address by Mandela at unveiling of Gandhi Memorial. Accessed at http://www.mandela.gov.za/mandela_speeches/1993/930606_gandhi.htm*
12. *Das, Durga (1970), "India: From Curzon to Nehru and After" pp. 155, Collins, London*
13. *"Selected Works of Jawaharlal Nehru" Vol. 3, pp. 134, Ed. By . Gopal, Jawaharlal Nehru Memorial Fund*
14. *"Selected Works of Jawaharlal Nehru" Vol. 3, pp. 98, Ed. By. Gopal, Jawaharlal Nehru Memorial Fund*
15. *Matthews, Roderick "Jinnah vs Gandhi" pp. 282, Hachette India*
16. *Gupta, Manju (2013): A Comparative Study of Three Legendary Men. Accessed at https://organiser.org/2013/01/19/52900/general/r1f631fc3/*
17. *Lapierre, Dominique and Larry Collins (1975): Freedom at Midnight,pp. 198, William Collins, UK*
18. *Hajari, Nisid (2015), "Midnight's Furies: The Deadly Legacy of India's Partition" pp. 4, Houghton Mifflin Harcourt*
19. *Pirazada, SyedSharifuddin (1984), "Collected Works of Quais-e-Azam Mohammad Ali Jinnah" pp. 421, East and West Publishing Company*
20. *Gandhi, M.K. "The Collected Works of Mahatama Gandhi" Vol. 78, pp. 386, Gandhi Sevagram Ashram*
21. *Pyarelal (1956): Mahatma Gandhi: The Last Phase: Vol 1, p. 303, Navjivan Publishing House, Ahmedabad*
22. *Gandhi, M.K. "The Collected Works of Mahatama Gandhi" Vol. 92, pp.*

344, Gandhi Sevagram Ashram

23. Gandhi, M.K. "The Collected Works of Mahatama Gandhi" Vol. 92, pp. 355, Gandhi Sevagram Ashram
24. Gandhi, M.K. "The Collected Works of Mahatama Gandhi" Vol. 76, pp. 356, Gandhi Sevagram Ashram
25. Obama, Barack (2020): A Promised Land,Crown Publishers, New York
26. Ibid
27. Fox, Richard G. (1987): 'Gandhian Socialism and Hindu Nationalism: Cultural Domination in the World System', Journal of Commonwealth and Comparative Politics, p. 233

□

Annexure-1

The Lahore Resolution

Resolved at the Lahore Session of All-India Muslim League held on March 22nd-24th, 1940.

(1) While approving and endorsing the action taken by the Council and the Working Committee of the All Indian Muslim League as indicated in their resolutions dated the 27th of August, 17th and 18th of September and 22nd of October, 1939, and February 3, 1940 on the constitutional issues, this Session of the All-Indian Muslim League emphatically reiterates that the scheme of federation embodied in the Government of India Act, 1935, is totally unsuited to, and unworkable in the peculiar conditions of this country and is altogether unacceptable to Muslim India.

(2) Resolved that it is the considered view of this Session of the All India Muslim League that no constitutional plan would be workable in this country or acceptable to Muslims unless it is designed on the following basic principle, namely that geographically contiguous units are demarcated into regions which should be so constituted, with such territorial readjustments as may be necessary, that the areas in which the Muslims are numerically in a majority as in the North-Western and Eastern Zones of India, should be grouped to constitute "Independent States" in which the constituent

units shall be autonomous and sovereign.

(3) That adequate, effective and mandatory safeguards should be specifically provided in the constitution for minorities in these units and in these regions for the protection of their religious, cultural, economic, political, administrative and other rights and interests in consultation with them; and in other parts of India where the Mussalmans are in a minority, adequate, effective and mandatory safeguards shall be specially provided in the constitution for them and other minorities for the protection of their religious, cultural, economic, political, administrative and other rights and interests in consultation with them.

(4) This Session further authorizes the Working Committee to frame a scheme of constitution in accordance with these basic principles, providing for the assumption finally by the respective regions of all powers such as defense, external affairs, communications, customs and such other matters as may be necessary."

□

Annexure-2

Quit India Resolution As Proposed by Gandhi

Whereas the British War Cabinet proposals by Sir Stafford Cripps have shown up British imperialism in its nakedness as never before, the All-India Congress Committee has come to the following conclusions:

The committee is of the opinion that Britain is incapable of defending India. It is natural that whatever she does is for her own defense. There is the eternal conflict between Indian and British interest. It follows that their notions of defense would also differ.

The British Government has no trust in India's political parties. The Indian Army has been maintained up till now mainly to hold India in subjugation. It has been completely segregated from the general population, who can in no sense regard it as their own. This policy of mistrust still continues, and is the reason why national defense is not entrusted to India's elected representatives.

Japan's quarrel is not with India. She is warring against the British Empire. India's participation in the war has not been with the consent of the representatives of the Indian people. It was purely a British act. If India were freed, her first step would probably be to negotiate with Japan.

Defense is Held Possible

The Congress is of the opinion that if the British withdrew from India, India would be able to defend herself in the event of the Japanese, or any aggressor, attacking India.

The committee is, therefore, of the opinion that the British should withdraw from India. The plea that they should remain in India for the protection of the Indian princes is wholly untenable. It is an additional proof of their determination to maintain their hold over India. The princes need have no fear from an unarmed India.

The question of majority and minority is the creation of the British Government, and would disappear on their withdrawal.

For all these reasons, the committee appeals to Britain, for the sake of her own safety, for the sake of India's safety and for the cause of world peace, to let go her hold on India, even if she does not give up all her Asiatic and African possessions.

This committee desires to assure the Japanese Government and people that India bears no enmity, either toward Japan or toward any other nation. India only desires freedom from all alien domination. But in this fight for freedom the committee is of the opinion that India, while welcoming universal sympathy, does not stand in need of foreign military aid.

Policy of Non-Cooperation

India will attain her freedom through her non-violent strength, and will retain it likewise. Therefore, the committee hopes that Japan will not have any designs on India. But if

Japan attacks India, and Britain makes no response to its appeal, the committee will expect all those who look to the Congress for guidance to offer complete non-violent non-cooperation to the Japanese forces, and not to render any assistance to them. It is no part of the duty of those who are attacked to render any assistance to the attacker. It is their duty to offer complete non-cooperation.

It is not difficult to understand the simple principle of nonviolent non-cooperation:

First, we may not bend the knee to an aggressor, or obey any of his orders.

Second, we may not look to him for any favors nor fall to his bribes, but we may not bear him any malice nor wish him ill.

Third, if he wishes to take possession of our fields we will refuse to give them up, even if we have to die in an effort to resist him.

Fourth, if he is attacked by disease, or is dying of thirst and seeks our aid, we may not refuse it.

Fifth, in such places where British and Japanese forces are fighting, our non-cooperation will be fruitless and unnecessary.

Non-Cooperation Limited

At present, our non-cooperation with the British Government is limited. Were we to offer them complete non-cooperation when they are actually fighting, it would be tantamount to bringing our country deliberately into Japanese hands. Therefore, not to put any obstacle in the way of the British forces will often be the only way of demonstrating our non-cooperation with the Japanese.

Neither may we assist the British in any active manner. If we can judge from their recent attitude, the British Government do not need any help from us beyond our non-interference. They desire our help only as slaves.

It is not necessary for the committee to make a clear declaration in regard to a scorched-earth policy. If, in spite of our nonviolence, any part of the country falls into Japanese hands, we may not destroy our crops or water supply, etc., if only because it will be our endeavor to regain them. The destruction of war material is another matter, and may, under certain circumstances, be a military necessity. But it can never be the Congress policy to destroy what belongs, or is of use, to the masses.

Says That All Must Work

Whilst non-cooperation against the Japanese forces will necessarily be limited to a comparatively small number, and must succeed if it is complete and genuine, true building up of swaraj [self-government] consists in the millions of India wholeheartedly working for a constructive program. Without it, the whole nation cannot rise from its age-long torpor.

Whether the British remain or not, it is our duty always to wipe out our unemployment, to bridge the gulf between the rich and the poor, to banish communal strife, to exorcise the demon of untouchability, to reform the Dacoits [armed bandits] and save the people from them. If scores of people do not take a living interest in this nation-building work, freedom must remain a dream and unattainable by either non-violence or violence.

Foreign soldiers: The committee is of the opinion that

it is harmful to India's interests, and dangerous to the cause of India's freedom, to introduce foreign soldiers in India. It therefore appeals to the British Government to remove these foreign legions, and henceforth stop further introduction. It is a crying shame to bring foreign troops in, in spite of India's inexhaustible man power, and it is proof of the immorality that British imperialism is.

□

Index

A

B

C

K

L

T

U

V

W

Y

Z